Learning AWS OpsWorks

Learn how to exploit advanced technologies to
deploy and auto-scale web stacks

Todd Rosner

PUBLISHING

BIRMINGHAM - MUMBAI

Learning AWS OpsWorks

First published: September 2013

Production Reference: 1130913

Published by Packt Publishing Ltd.
Livery Place
35 Livery Street
Birmingham B3 2PB, UK.

ISBN 978-1-78217-110-2

www.packtpub.com

Cover Image by Žarko Piljak (zpiljak@gmail.com)

Credits

Author
Todd Rosner

Reviewers
Nils De Moor

Tom O'Connor

Thomas Goddard

Acquisition Editor
Usha Iyer

Commissioning Editor
Poonam Jain

Technical Editors
Dylan Fernandes

Monica John

Project Coordinator
Amey Sawant

Proofreader
Lauren Harkins

Indexer
Priya Subramani

Graphics
Ronak Dhruv

Production Coordinator
Manu Joseph

Cover Work
Manu Joseph

About the Author

Todd Rosner is a technologist with over 12 years of related industry experience. Through this experience Todd has fulfilled several roles which include computer development, network engineering, Internet application development, and cloud computing.

Todd is currently the proprietor of Vivisurf; a consulting agency that assists companies in understanding and working with the complexities of cloud computing and Internet application development. Todd is also an affiliate of an Internet startup called yodilly, a platform that enables publishers to monetize content using curated commerce.

Todd can be reached via Twitter as `@toddrosner` and by inquiring through `http://www.vivisurf.com`

About the Reviewers

Nils De Moor is a developer living in Belgium. He has a deep interest in developing applications in distributed environments. After he graduated from the University of Antwerp, he went on to start a PhD research position in the fields of simulating distributed computing systems and the financial efficiency of allocating resources.

Later on, he worked for the Belgian railways and one of the biggest telecoms companies in the country to finally start a SaaS platform called WooRank, with his 2 friends. This startup builds a tool for digital marketing companies to generate reports and keep an eye on the online presence of their clients and prospects. This platform gave him broad experience in running and upscaling huge workloads across a robust infrastructure.

Nils has contributed as a writer to an academical paper, titled *Scalability of Grid Simulators: An Evaluation*. He is also highly active in the AWS community and is the main organizer of the Belgian AWS User Group.

Tom O'Connor is an experienced systems architect and DevOps engineer, living in the West Midlands in the United Kingdom. Over the last eight years, Tom has worked in a wide variety of companies, from e-commerce to video effects, and now owns his own company, providing systems consultancy for wireless network design and installations.

Tom writes a technical blog on his website, providing both tutorial articles and updates on what he's been working on. He has wide-reaching skills and experience gathered over the last 10 years, having worked on Windows, Linux, and Unix systems for most of that time, coupled with recent experience in designing and building high-performance computer systems.

Tom is also an active member of the UK DevOps community, as well as a community moderator on `ServerFault.com`, where he demonstrates his expertise and skills to a wide audience.

This is the first book Tom has officially reviewed, and he would like to consider becoming a technical author in the coming months.

www.PacktPub.com

Support files, eBooks, discount offers and more

You might want to visit www.PacktPub.com for support files and downloads related to your book.

Did you know that Packt offers eBook versions of every book published, with PDF and ePub files available? You can upgrade to the eBook version at www.PacktPub.com and as a print book customer, you are entitled to a discount on the eBook copy. Get in touch with us at service@packtpub.com for more details.

At www.PacktPub.com, you can also read a collection of free technical articles, sign up for a range of free newsletters and receive exclusive discounts and offers on Packt books and eBooks.

http://PacktLib.PacktPub.com

Do you need instant solutions to your IT questions? PacktLib is Packt's online digital book library. Here, you can access, read and search across Packt's entire library of books.

Why Subscribe?

- Fully searchable across every book published by Packt
- Copy and paste, print and bookmark content
- On demand and accessible via web browser

Free Access for Packt account holders

If you have an account with Packt at www.PacktPub.com, you can use this to access PacktLib today and view nine entirely free books. Simply use your login credentials for immediate access.

Instant Updates on New Packt Books

Get notified! Find out when new books are published by following @PacktEnterprise on Twitter, or the *Packt Enterprise* Facebook page.

Table of Contents

Preface

AWS OpsWorks is a Chef Framework solution for application and infrastructure management. Using AWS OpsWorks, DevOps teams can systematically manage, deploy, and scale global infrastructures and applications faster, and with much less effort in comparison to methods which have been previously used.

Learning AWS OpsWorks covers basic, intermediate, and advanced features and concepts as they relate to OpsWorks. This book will not only teach you about OpsWorks, but you will gain valuable information about key concepts such as load balancing, auto scaling, multistage environments, and so on. You will also learn how these key concepts relate to OpsWorks, and how they can be used to assist with scaling web applications.

This book starts by introducing you to the fundamentals of the technology, and how to get involved with Amazon Web Services (AWS). *Learning AWS OpsWorks* then moves on to working with major components known as stacks, layers, instances, and apps. You will also learn how to set up detailed monitoring, and how to configure and work with access control, and perform command-line reporting. Finally, it will provide information about taking OpsWorks to the next level with multi-region architecture.

If you are looking for a book that will enable you to quickly and easily get up and running with AWS OpsWorks for managing applications of any scale on the AWS cloud, then this book is for you.

What this book covers

Chapter 1, A New Way to Scale explains that OpsWorks is a tool that was designed by a third party company with the goal of making it easier to both integrate and scale AWS services using Chef. AWS recognized this tool as a bit of a game changer, then acquired the technology so that they could bring even tighter integration with native services to allow a DevOps team the ability to configure, deploy, manage, and scale infrastructure and applications easily using the AWS cloud.

Chapter 2, Welcome to AWS OpsWorks describes that creating an AWS account is not only easy, but also gives you access to all of the AWS services that are available in the AWS Management Console. The AWS Management Console provides access to the OpsWorks dashboard where you can gain access to documentation, learn about what's new, as well as create stacks as high-level containers for the items discussed in the following chapters.

Chapter 3, Stack it Up! is an introduction to the concept of multistage environments and how those are represented in OpsWorks as something called stacks. This chapter covers creating a stack, the available parameters, and how to work with functions that allow for stack management.

Chapter 4, Layers – The Blueprint for Success provides information about the different types of layers, and how the Chef framework works with respect to built-in Chef and custom Chef recipes. This chapter also discusses ELB, EBS, EIP, OS packages, security groups, IAM instance profiles, and auto healing within the context of working with layers.

Chapter 5, In an Instance takes a look at the different instance types that are available to OpsWorks, as well as the various scaling types that can be applied to those instances. A load-based scaling array is defined and instances are added to it for the purpose of auto scaling in response to traffic demand.

Chapter 6, Bring the Apps! shows that application development software and methods such as IDE and Git are essential for any system that intends to scale. Coordinating local development with version control systems and the creation of apps is really the only way to achieve application deployments using OpsWorks.

Chapter 7, Big Brother covers ways in which OpsWorks provides monitoring for stacks, layers, and instances, and how CloudWatch is integrated. The OpsWorks graphing system has a clean and simple layout, and it delivers point-in-time views that are easy to navigate and easy to understand.

Chapter 8, Access Control introduces AWS Identity and Access Management and demonstrates how IAM integrates with OpsWorks for securing infrastructure and applications.

Chapter 9, Instance Agent CLI provides information about how command-line reports can be run for retrieving information about the configuration and status of different elements within the OpsWorks framework.

Chapter 10, Multi-region Architecture covers the next logical step in web-scale architecture using OpsWorks—Multi-region Architecture. In addition, this chapter also provides information about the qualities and benefits of using Route 53 for managing DNS in relation to multi-region architecture.

What you need for this book

This book assumes that the reader has some awareness of AWS, integrated development environments, version control systems, and configuration management. Requirements for this book include an OpsWorks-enabled AWS account, a local integrated development environment (preferably with Sublime Text 2 on OS X), and Git for version control, as well as a GitHub account for VCS hosting. Ubuntu Linux 12.04 LTS will be the working operating system for all instances created throughout the chapters of this book.

Who this book is for

Ideally written for the startup, this book is geared toward application developers, system administrators, DevOps, and anyone else interested in delivering applications while managing highly scalable and automated infrastructures using AWS.

Conventions

In this book, you will find a number of styles of text that distinguish between different kinds of information. Here are some examples of these styles, and an explanation of their meaning.

Code words in text are shown as follows: "We can include other contexts through the use of the `include` directive."

A block of code is set as follows:

```
[default]
exten => s,1,Dial(Zap/1|30)
exten => s,2,Voicemail(u100)
exten => s,102,Voicemail(b100)
exten => i,1,Voicemail(s0)
```

When we wish to draw your attention to a particular part of a code block, the relevant lines or items are set in bold:

```
[default]
exten => s,1,Dial(Zap/1|30)
exten => s,2,Voicemail(u100)
exten => s,102,Voicemail(b100)
exten => i,1,Voicemail(s0)
```

Any command-line input or output is written as follows:

```
# cp /usr/src/asterisk-addons/configs/cdr_mysql.conf.sample
    /etc/asterisk/cdr_mysql.conf
```

New terms and **important words** are shown in bold. Words that you see on the screen, in menus or dialog boxes for example, appear in the text like this: "clicking the **Next** button moves you to the next screen".

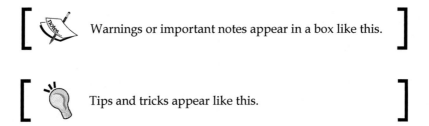

Warnings or important notes appear in a box like this.

Tips and tricks appear like this.

Reader feedback

Feedback from our readers is always welcome. Let us know what you think about this book—what you liked or may have disliked. Reader feedback is important for us to develop titles that you really get the most out of.

To send us general feedback, simply send an e-mail to feedback@packtpub.com, and mention the book title via the subject of your message.

If there is a topic that you have expertise in and you are interested in either writing or contributing to a book, see our author guide on www.packtpub.com/authors.

Customer support

Now that you are the proud owner of a Packt book, we have a number of things to help you to get the most from your purchase.

Errata

Although we have taken every care to ensure the accuracy of our content, mistakes do happen. If you find a mistake in one of our books—maybe a mistake in the text or the code—we would be grateful if you would report this to us. By doing so, you can save other readers from frustration and help us improve subsequent versions of this book. If you find any errata, please report them by visiting http://www.packtpub.com/submit-errata, selecting your book, clicking on the **errata submission form** link, and entering the details of your errata. Once your errata are verified, your submission will be accepted and the errata will be uploaded on our website, or added to any list of existing errata, under the Errata section of that title. Any existing errata can be viewed by selecting your title from http://www.packtpub.com/support.

Piracy

Piracy of copyright material on the Internet is an ongoing problem across all media. At Packt, we take the protection of our copyright and licenses very seriously. If you come across any illegal copies of our works, in any form, on the Internet, please provide us with the location address or website name immediately so that we can pursue a remedy.

Please contact us at copyright@packtpub.com with a link to the suspected pirated material.

We appreciate your help in protecting our authors, and our ability to bring you valuable content.

Questions

You can contact us at questions@packtpub.com if you are having a problem with any aspect of the book, and we will do our best to address it.

1
A New Way to Scale

This chapter provides a high-level look at what AWS OpsWorks is, where OpsWorks came from, why it came to be, and why the service is important. One of the key drivers behind OpsWorks is something called DevOps, which you may or may not be aware of. In this chapter, we will take a quick look at the DevOps role, and also explain who will benefit the most from using OpsWorks.

High-level OpsWorks

As you may have guessed from the title, this book is about AWS OpsWorks and how it can be put to practical use so that web applications can scale with minimal effort. OpsWorks is a Chef Framework solution for application and infrastructure management. Using AWS OpsWorks, DevOps teams can systematically manage, deploy, and scale global infrastructures and applications faster, and with much less effort in comparison to previously used methods.

OpsWorks is one of the many services provided by **Amazon Web Services (AWS)**. The thing that stands out about OpsWorks is that it allows you to bootstrap complete environments that contain other AWS services. For example, with OpsWorks, AWS services such as EC2, ELB, EBS, Elastic IP, Security Groups, Route 53, CloudWatch, and IAM can all play a part in its configuration.

Managing the configuration of several services at once and in advance provides for automated deployment of applications and the infrastructure that supports them. Accessing OpsWorks involves having an AWS account, then navigating to it using the AWS Management Console by going to **Deployment & Management | OpsWorks** as shown in the following screenshot:

To date, OpsWorks has four defining areas which all work together in providing configuration management for scaling web applications. These areas are briefly defined in the following paragraphs.

Stacks

At the highest level, OpsWorks uses something called **stacks**. There are many possible uses for this high-level item, and one such use could be as a stage within a multistage environment (think test, staging, production, and so on.); a single stack could represent the staging environment. In the example of a stack called staging, the stack would serve as a container, which includes configuration settings for enabling layers, instances, and apps.

Layers

The second level of OpsWorks is called **layers**. A layer is a blueprint for EC2 instances, EBS volumes, load balancers and so on, which function in a specific way. Layers define which packages and applications are installed, and how they are configured. An example of a layer is a Rails app server. The Rails app server includes configuration items such as the Ruby version, (which Rails stack to use), the RubyGems version, and whether or not to manage a particular version of Bundler.

Instances

At the third tier, OpsWorks provides a method for launching and managing **instances**. Instances are the EC2 instances that serve applications and data, balance traffic, and so on, in accordance to the configuration of their parent layer. As instances are launched, they will show up in the EC2 section of the AWS Management Console.

Apps

At the fourth level of OpsWorks are the **apps**. An app is application code that you want to run on an instance. Apps hold configuration information, which is required to deploy application code to application server instances. With an app, you define what code base it is (PHP), where it resides (GitHub), and what domain names it should be associated with.

The origin of OpsWorks

AWS OpsWorks wasn't always a part of AWS. Actually, OpsWorks was originally a product called Scalarium, which was created in July 2008 by Berlin-based startup Peritor. AWS acquired Peritor in 2012, which then launched a modified version of Scalarium called OpsWorks in February 2013. AWS then discontinued Scalarium in August 2013, while providing a migration path for its existing customers up until that point. Founders of Peritor Scalarium included Thomas Metschke, Jonathan Weiss, and Mathias Meyer.

AWS recognized that Scalarium had strong capabilities that were broadly useful to AWS customers, and they've done an excellent job to date in transitioning and building upon the new service. As AWS continues to rapidly deploy new services and features, one can only assume that OpsWorks will eventually be tied into the majority of them.

The importance of OpsWorks

So, you might still be asking yourself how and why OpsWorks is important anyway. Good question!

OpsWorks is important for several reasons. First, OpsWorks is a service native to AWS and because of this, it works seamlessly with other AWS services that it supports. Status information and callback response with services such as EC2, ELB, EIP, CloudWatch and so on, are updated in real time. This means that as changes are initiated to infrastructure, callbacks to the OpsWorks console happen immediately so that users don't have to wait for status updates prior to moving forward with other changes or additions.

Secondly, OpsWorks provides the ability to create full stacks, which can then be cloned into other stacks. This is extremely efficient for infrastructure development. For example, it allows individuals in a DevOps role to build a complete staging stack that includes layers and instances which are configured using Chef, then clone it to production, and then with the click of a button, bring an entire production environment, including applications, online within minutes.

Another very important aspect of OpsWorks is **auto scaling**. Auto scaling allows you to scale EC2 capacity up or down automatically according to predefined conditions. With auto scaling, it's possible to ensure that the number of Amazon EC2 instances you're using increases seamlessly during demand spikes to maintain performance, and decreases automatically during demand lulls to minimize costs.

Auto scaling is particularly well-suited to applications that experience hourly, daily, or weekly variability in usage. With OpsWorks, there are two distinct auto scaling options: time-based and load-based. This practically allows any flexibility with auto scaling that a DevOps team might require in meeting the demands of a rapidly growing business.

One other important feature of OpsWorks is application deployment. OpsWorks can be configured to automatically deploy application code from source code repositories hosted in Git and Subversion repositories, as well as S3 and HTTP archives. Members of a DevOps team can update code in a repository or archive, and then deploy the updates simultaneously across all application servers with the click of a button. This is a very powerful feature that solves the problem of maintaining code version consistency across servers.

Yet another very important feature of OpsWorks is **disaster recovery (DR)**. With OpsWorks, systems can be architected so that they're region agnostic. This means that an entire network of instances can span multiple regions and also multiple zones within the AWS cloud. In this type of a configuration, an entire AWS Region could fail and a business application can continue to run. **Auto healing**, which exists at the layer level, is another DR feature of OpsWorks. When auto healing is enabled, instances can fail and OpsWorks will automatically replace them in their entirety.

The role of DevOps

DevOps...that term that is being thrown around these days. **DevOps**, a portmanteau of **Development and Operations**, is typically a software development methodology that stresses communication, collaboration, and integration between Development, Technology Operations, and Quality Assurance. There are varying ways of how this method is implemented, and in the case of AWS OpsWorks, DevOps refers to a team of individuals that has experience with all three facets of the business at hand. The following figure is an illustration of how the DevOps method is ideally situated:

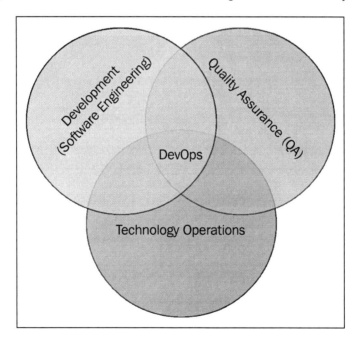

In this scenario, a DevOps team communicates with Developers and Quality Assurance to ensure that application code is ready to be released to the servers that support it. DevOps can then deploy the code using the OpsWorks deployment features. DevOps also plays a role in communicating with Operations to ensure that the infrastructure in question effectively supports the application code that Developers are working on.

OpsWorks for the startup

Internet startups that are looking toward rapid growth and scaling should consider OpsWorks as the platform for their applications. With OpsWorks, businesses including startups can look forward to the following for powering and protecting their infrastructure and applications:

- Bootstrapped learning through familiarity with AWS
- Tight integration with other Amazon Web Services
- The ability to easily build and deploy distinct system environments, that is; test, staging, and production
- Fine grained control over infrastructure
- Infrastructure auto scaling
- Automatic deployment of application code across many servers
- Disaster recovery through intelligent architecture and auto healing

As you can see, any organization including Internet startups that are looking to effectively deploy, manage, and scale their infrastructure and application code will benefit from the use of OpsWorks. As the two worlds of System Engineers and Developers continue to meld, services like OpsWorks will become increasingly prevalent. For any other requirements that don't involve the previously mentioned elements, simply using the EC2 console for launching and managing individual EC2 instances, EBS volumes, EIPs, and so on will suffice.

Summary

OpsWorks is a tool that was designed by a third-party company with the goal of making it easier to both integrate and scale AWS services using Chef. AWS recognized this tool as a bit of a game changer, and then acquired the technology so that they could bring even tighter integration with native services to allow a DevOps team the ability to configure, deploy, manage, and scale infrastructure and applications easily using the AWS cloud.

In the next chapter, we will get acquainted with AWS and OpsWorks by walking through the setup of an AWS account, and then move on to the OpsWorks dashboard.

2
Welcome to AWS OpsWorks

This chapter moves straight into explaining and showing you how to create an AWS account, if you don't already have one. After you've created an AWS account, this chapter will show you how to get to the OpsWorks dashboard, and will explain a bit about what you will find once you get there.

Creating an AWS account

Because, AWS OpsWorks is a part of AWS, one of its requirements is, of course, an AWS account. If you already have an AWS account and are familiar with other AWS services, feel free to skip to the next section titled *The Dashboard*.

If you don't yet have an AWS account setup, head on over to aws.amazon.com and click on the **Get Started for Free** button to get started today. Sign up for AWS by filling in your desired e-mail address and selecting **I am a new user**, and then click on the **Sign in using our secure server** button.

> When creating a new AWS account for business purposes, it's generally a good idea to create a new e-mail address such as AWS@domain.tld for its use. Even though Amazon IAM provides a great way to distinguish accounts, it's possible that these credentials will be used by other individuals in your organization, so you'll want this to be something that is non-personal. You should also create a very strong (20 characters) and randomized password to go with it.

An example of the sign up process can be seen in the following screenshots:

Once you've completed this step, you will be presented with another form for more details surrounding your account. Fill in the required information and click on the **Continue** button:

My name is:	Your Name
My e-mail address is:	AWS@domain.tld
Type it again:	AWS@domain.tld

note: this is the e-mail address that we will use to contact you about your account

Enter a new password:	••••••••••••••••••••
Type it again:	••••••••••••••••••••

Continue ▶

Enter in all of the information for the fields on the following page:

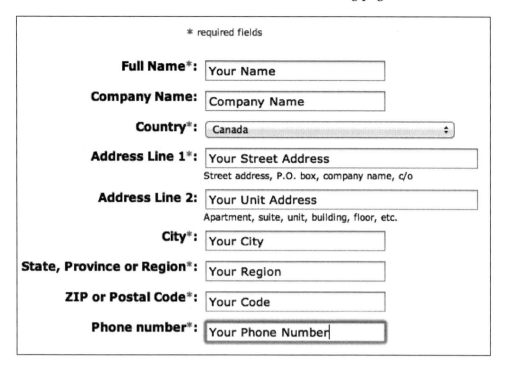

Fill in the characters as displayed in the following Captcha image:

Check the **Terms of Service** checkbox, and then click on the **Create Account and Continue** button.

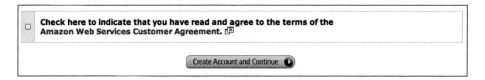

Once you see the thank you message and have confirmed that your account is created, access the AWS Management Console and navigate to AWS OpsWorks by navigating **Services** | **Deployment & Management** | **AWS OpsWorks**.

The dashboard

The OpsWorks dashboard is fairly basic prior to any configuration; it provides a detailed explanation of what OpsWorks is, and includes a feature overview and a basic instructional video.

The dashboard also provides access to documentation and any new features that have recently been released. At the time of this writing, OpsWorks has just added support for more EC2 instance types and Elastic Load Balancing, as well as a new view for CloudWatch.

The following image gives an example of what to expect when accessing the OpsWorks dashboard for the very first time:

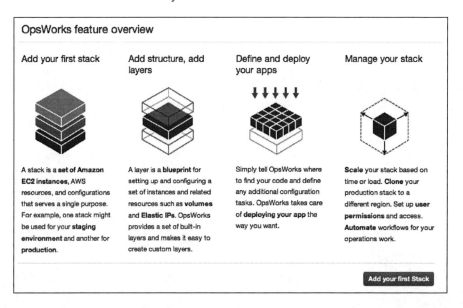

As soon as the first stack is created, the OpsWorks feature overview is replaced by a layout that includes the created stacks. This provides a user with the ability to have a quick understanding of all environments (test, staging, and production) as they relate to applications. The dashboard will also include functions for managing stacks as they are created.

Summary

Creating an AWS account is not only easy, but it also gives you access to all of the AWS services that are available in the AWS Management Console. Using the AWS Management Console, there is a quick link to OpsWorks under the Deployment and Management section. The OpsWorks link will take you straight into the OpsWorks dashboard where you can gain access to documentation and learn about what's new, as well as create stacks as high-level containers for the items discussed in the following chapters.

In the next chapter, we will dive right into the top-level item of OpsWorks called **stacks**. *Chapter 3, Stack it Up!* will cover all of the elements of a stack, and will provide information about multistage environments as they relate to OpsWorks and stacks.

3
Stack it Up!

This chapter takes the next step with OpsWorks by configuring stacks. A stack represents a fully controlled environment for deployment or test-driven development. This chapter will provide an insight about the concepts of multistage environments, and how an OpsWorks stack factors into that.

Multistage environments

The concept of having a multistage environment is a very important one. Obviously, one should not perform code and infrastructure changes to a live system without testing things out first. To allow for proper testing of changes to code and infrastructure, separate systems need to be provided; those systems are typically named development, test, staging, and production. This is accurately referred to as a multistage environment.

For the purpose of this book and its readers, we will be focusing on a three tier multistage environment that includes development, staging, and production. Each tier or environment that exists within a multistage environment is referred to as a stack in OpsWorks.

Development environment

The development environment is something that would typically exist in a distributed nature outside of OpsWorks. **Local Integrated Development Environments (Local IDE)** should be created on each developer's notebook. This includes things such as application middleware, web servers, database servers, Memcached, and so on. The localized code repository should be initialized using Git, and then pushed to a private or public repository on GitHub or something similar. Using a distributed VCS such as Git with GitHub provides code redundancy and the ability to carry your code with you and work on it anywhere, as well as the ability to create branches which other developers can then test and add or modify. We will not be covering Git in this book, as it is an advanced VCS which takes some real research and understanding to use. However, once you're up and running with Git, you won't want to turn back. For that reason, it is highly encouraged that all developers learn to use Git.

Staging environment

The staging environment should almost be an exact mirror of the production environment you wish to deploy, depending on scale. For this reason, it's advisable that you build the staging environment first, work with it, and tune to the point where it has all of the elements for production, including excellent performance, and then clone it into a production environment. If you plan on having a vast array of proxy, application, database servers, and so on for your production environment, you can probably start out a bit smaller for the staging environment, clone it to production, and then add more server arrays to production after.

For example, if you plan on having 10 application servers and 4 database servers for production, you can safely provision 2 or 3 application servers and a couple of database servers for staging. The staging environment is also often used for QA testing, should there be the absence of an actual testing environment.

Production environment

The production environment is obviously the golden child of all environments, and it should be treated with extreme care. Production should be configured to allow for auto scaling, and then left untouched once everything is deployed. Any required code or infrastructure changes should be initially tested using development and staging, which can then be pushed or updated to production. It is very advisable to also prepare auto scaling on staging, and then to load test this environment with the goal of understanding initial scale requirements.

Now, if you are familiar with multistage environments, you may be asking yourself, "What about the test environment?" The test environment has traditionally been important and has enabled quality assurance engineers the ability to work on a system to test changes before they are pushed to the staging environment. This is a bit of an overly cautious approach, but it does have some merit with certain situations, applications, and infrastructure.

Automated build environment

Recently, there have been a lot of advances with automated build systems so that developers can get their code to production as quickly as possible. In many situations, this has eliminated the test environment by allowing developers to push their code through a build system that automatically runs quality checks, which will either pass or fail. If the code passes, the developer can push to staging (which is a mirror copy of production), any further QA can be done on staging with respect to both the code and infrastructure, and then the code can be pushed to production.

Adding a stack

When you access the OpsWorks dashboard, you should see a button that says **Add stack**. For this book and the benefit of its readers, we're going to go ahead and create a stack called **Staging**. The staging stack will represent a staging environment, which can later be cloned into production once configured how we want it to be.

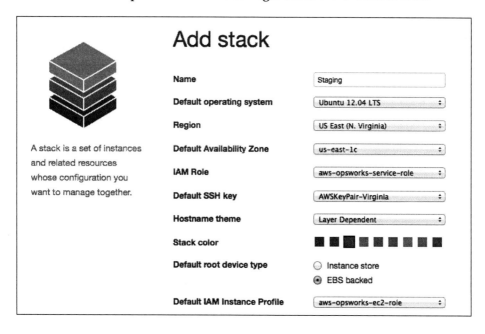

Name the stack **Staging**. Now, there are several options available to you for configuring a stack; the first of which is the **Default operating system**. OpsWorks provides two options here, **Amazon Linux** and **Ubuntu 12.04 LTS**. Amazon Linux is based on CentOS and is designed to have excellent performance on the AWS virtualization platform. As excellent as Amazon Linux is, in many respects, Ubuntu is even better because of its package availability and the way in which those packages are configured by default. Aside from that, Ubuntu also has excellent performance on AWS and a nice Bash color scheme.

Go ahead and select **Ubuntu 12.04 LTS** as the **Default operating system** for the staging stack.

Regions

Next up is the region selection. A region in AWS is a separate geographic area, such as US East—Virginia, US West—Northern California, EU Ireland, and so on. Each region has multiple, isolated locations known as availability zones. AWS provides you with the ability to place resources, such as instances, and data in multiple availability zones and regions. Select **US East (N. Virginia)** as the region.

 The US East—Virginia region receives new services and service updates before any of the other regions.

Availability zones

As mentioned in the previous paragraph, regions consist of availability zones. An availability zone is a physically distinct and independent infrastructure, which is engineered to be highly reliable. Common points of failure like generators and cooling equipment are not shared across availability zones. Additionally, availability zones are also physically separate so that extreme disasters such as fires, tornados, or flooding do not affect more than a single zone at any one time. At this time, there are capacity constraints for some instance types within us-east-1a and us-east-1b. Choose **us-east-1c** as the **Default Availability Zone**. If when reading this, **us-east-1c** also has capacity constraints, choose one of the remaining options.

IAM roles

OpsWorks support for IAM is based around the idea of roles. Configuring roles provides users and services access to OpsWorks without having to provide access to other dependent services such as EC2. For example, you can explicitly deny a user the ability to perform EC2 actions through the EC2 Management Console while still allowing control of EC2 instances through OpsWorks.

IAM roles are defined using JSON-based permissions, and this is a layer which we won't be covering in detail, so for this section, simply choose the default IAM role **aws-opsworks-service-role**.

Default SSH key

Next, select the Default SSH key to be used. This is something that you should have already created as soon as your AWS account was created. If you have not yet created an SSH key, head over to the EC2 section of the AWS Management Console to create one. Ideally, the name of the key should reflect the region that it is created in, that is, **AWSKeyPair-Virginia**. Once the SSH key is created, select the key as it is displayed beside the **Default SSH key** label.

> AWS generated SSH keys are not easy to recover if lost or misplaced. For this reason, it's incredibly important to secure and protect the SSH key once downloaded.

Hostname theme

Next, select the **Hostname theme**. The hostname theme is really just a fun way of having your instances named. Using the layer dependent theme is a very helpful and identifiable option, as it will automatically name your instances to reflect what they are, that is, **php-app1**. The other options present a level of entertainment, but at the same time they can cause some confusion when trying to address what they represent. Choose **Layer Dependent** as your **Hostname theme**.

Stack color

Select a stack color. There really isn't much reason for preference here, other than maybe you think that it makes sense for staging to be navy blue, and for production to be green. For the sake of this publication, choose navy blue for the staging stack color.

Advanced

Click on the **Advanced** hyperlink to display the advanced properties for this stack. These properties include things such as **Default root device type**, **Default IAM instance Profile**, whether to use **Custom Chef** and/or **Custom JSON**. We'll only go as far as defining the default root device type, in which case choose **EBS backed** instead of **instance store**.

EBS backed instances are much quicker at booting than instance store, and they allow for instances to be stopped and started instead of just terminated and re-launched.

 It's important to note here that if either instance is stopped or terminated; its entire configuration will be lost. Once the instance is again started, it will be reconfigured based on its layer.

OpsWorks should by default have already created a Default IAM instance Profile for you, which you can simply leave set as is. Once this stack is configured as described, click on the **Add stack** button.

Your staging stack is now created and you should see a screen similar to the following figure:

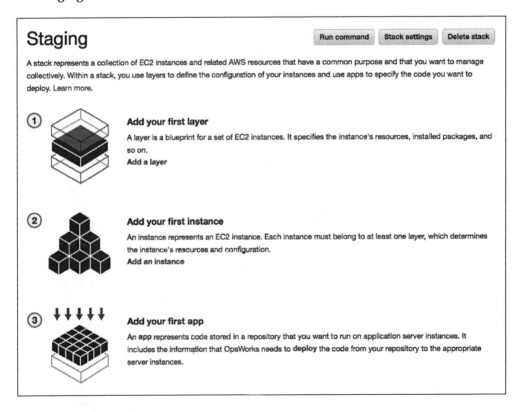

If you click on the **Dashboard** link in the top right corner of the OpsWorks console, you'll be taken to the dashboard. You should also notice that your staging stack is there. If you take a closer look, you'll notice that there's a link called **Actions** within the stack. If you click on this link, you'll see a drop-down that has **edit**, **start**, **clone**, and **delete** options.

We won't get into the functionality or details of these options just yet...that comes later. As the option names imply, **edit** is for editing an already existing stack, **start** is for bringing the entire stack online including all instances. The **clone** option is for cloning the stack, and is a very useful feature. For example, once the staging stack is configured as desired, it can simply be cloned to produce a new stack, which can then be named **production**.

> Once a stack is cloned, any further updates to it will not be synced to the newly cloned stack. The **delete** option is obviously for deleting a stack. In order to delete a stack, first the instances, apps, and layers must be deleted.

Inside the stack

Now, we've successfully created a staging stack and it's time to take a look at what's inside. As you're still in the OpsWorks dashboard, click on your staging stack to proceed. As you can see from the previous figure, there are quick links for adding layers, instances, and apps. Being that instances and apps are dependent on layers, we'll move ahead with creating a layer first. Go ahead and click on the **Add a layer** link to get started:

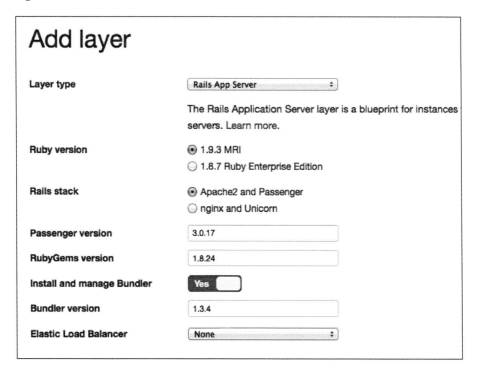

Layer types

At this point, you should be seeing something very similar to the previous figure. By default, OpsWorks displays options for a Rails application stack using either Apache2 with Passenger, or Nginx with Unicorn.

There are several options for building layers including HAProxy for high availability load balancing, Static Web Server such as Nginx or Varnish Cache, Rails App Server, PHP App Server, Node.js App Server, MySQL Database Server, Memcached key value store, and Ganglia for clustered monitoring. There's also an option to create a custom layer type, which will allow you to build almost anything you need. This option is designed for use with custom Chef and JSON, and if you have a Git repository that holds a series of Chef cookbooks, you can apply them to your custom layer to accomplish almost any server type you might need. This book only briefly goes over the subject of Chef, but it should be known that Chef is an integral component to OpsWorks.

For the purpose of this book, we're going to simplify things a bit and start out by creating a PHP application stack, then move onto adding an Elastic Load Balancer. Choose **PHP App Server** from the select list; take note that there is also an option for an ELB as illustrated in the following figure.

Add layer

Layer type	PHP App Server ⬍
	The PHP Application Server layer is a blueprint for instances By default PHP 5.3 and Apache 2.2 are installed. Learn more
Elastic Load Balancer	None ⬍

Elastic Load Balancer

If you try to choose an ELB, you'll notice that there probably isn't one available. We'll need to create an ELB, but before we do that, let's go over some details as to what an ELB is, and what it can accomplish.

The **Elastic Load Balancer**, or **ELB**, is AWS's load balancing solution. The ELB is a software-based load balancer that distributes traffic evenly to the EC2 instances that you're running. The ELB is a fully redundant solution that includes intelligence to avoid dead and overworked nodes as it scales request-handling capacity in response to incoming traffic.

For any single application, there's no need to provision more than one ELB per AWS Region. As simple and as effective as the ELB sounds, there are some points to be aware of, and these points could have some impact on your decision to use this load balancing service.

Algorithms

ELB provides **Round Robin (RR)** load-balancing and can include sticky session handling. There is no current ability to balance traffic based on at least connections or pre-determined weight using ELB, but these features could become available in the near future. If you currently require options of the latter, HAProxy will be your best alternative.

Protocols

ELB works with protocols such as HTTP, Secure HTTP, TCP, and Secure TCP. Using ELB, it's possible to terminate SSL at both the ELB and instances, thus providing full end-to-end encryption. ELB also works with the following ports: 25, 80, 443, and 1024-65535. If for some reason you do require available ports between 443 and 1024, HAProxy will be your best alternative.

Traffic spikes

ELB is designed to handle a very large number (20K+) of concurrent requests per second with a gradually increasing traffic pattern. ELB is not designed to handle sudden heavy spikes of traffic unless the ELB is pre-warmed first by consulting the AWS support team. If frequent sudden heavy spikes of traffic are anticipated for your application, HAProxy will be the better option.

Timeouts

ELB will timeout persistent socket connections after 60 seconds if left idle. This condition could present a problem if you are waiting for large files to be generated by a system that doesn't provide frequent callbacks.

HAProxy

HAProxy is an excellent alternative to ELB. HAProxy is designed for load balancing and it follows the UNIX philosophy of "do one thing and do it well". The use of HAProxy will allow you to overcome almost any constraint that ELB presents, with the exception of SSL termination.

Despite the fact that ELB ships with the earlier mentioned caveats, if HAProxy is used, both the financial and administration costs will be significantly higher. In order to maintain true high availability, redundant instances of HAProxy will have to be configured and managed. In order to support a massive pool of traffic with sudden spikes, m1.large instances at the very least, will be required. Scaling an infrastructure over multiple AWS regions is also much more of a challenge when using HAProxy.

ELB creation

Now that we've gained some information about ELB versus HAProxy, we'll move onto creating an ELB, then selecting it for our **PHP App Layer**. Move your mouse cursor over the ELB select box, but don't actually click on it. You should see a bit of text pop up that reads **Select an Elastic Load Balancer or add one**; click on the **add one** link to launch a new browser tab of the ELB section from the EC2 Management Console. Once the page loads, click on the **Create Load Balancer** button. A modal window should present itself as illustrated in the following screenshot:

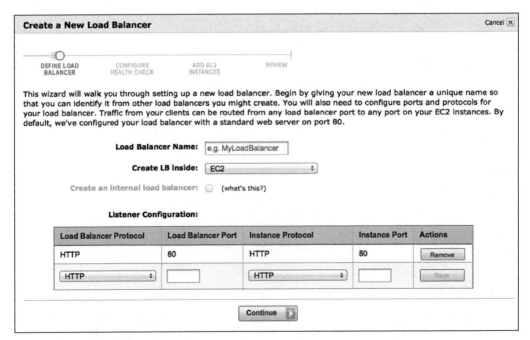

Give the load balancer a name. It's a good idea to name your ELB according to region, that is, LB-US-East. Select EC2 as the option for where to create the LB, and for the purpose of this writing, we're only going to keep the defaults of HTTP over port 80 as the listener.

As mentioned earlier, an ELB can be configured to terminate SSL over port 443, and then pass unencrypted traffic back to port 80 on the application servers. An ELB can also be configured to handle SSL over port 443, and then pass the encrypted traffic back to port 443 on the application servers, providing full end-to-end encryption.

Secure HTTP is a typically a requirement for any load balancer, but we're not going to go into the creation and configuration of self-signed SSL certificates to get Secure HTTP to work at this time.

Click on the **Continue** button. You should be presented with a modal window similar to the following figure:

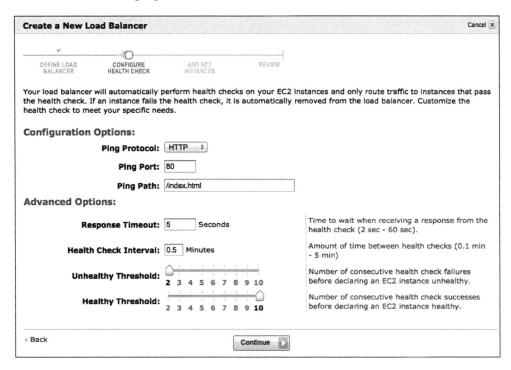

At this point, we can configure health checks for the EC2 instances that the ELB will be balancing traffic for. The default settings are acceptable for this exercise, but the one thing to actually consider is the **Ping Path**, which by default, is set to `index.html`. If your code is dynamic such as PHP, Ruby, or JavaScript, you'll want this to represent the index document supported by your code type, that is, `index.php`, and so on. Change this field to `/index.php`, and click on the **Continue** button.

The next modal window will give you the opportunity to add any already existing EC2 instances to your ELB. By selecting each instance, you will be shown the **Availability Zone Distribution**. When shown this, the ELB setup will tell you if you have even distribution or if you should configure additional EC2 instances in a separate zone to distribute traffic evenly over AWS zones. Because we're going to use this ELB with instances that will be created with OpsWorks, make sure to leave every instance unchecked if there are any. Click on the **Continue** button to proceed.

Review your configuration and then click on the **Create** button to create your ELB. This can take a few minutes to complete, and once done, head back to OpsWorks.

Now, if your ELB was successfully created, you should be able to close the **ELB** tab of your browser, then navigate to the **OpsWorks** tab and select the ELB for your PHP App Layer as illustrated in the following figure:

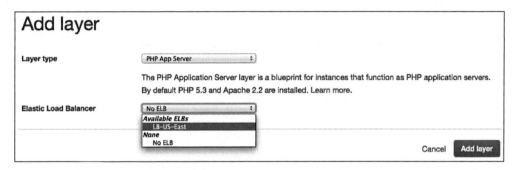

Select the ELB and click on the **Add layer** button to proceed. You should now see a page similar to what's displayed in the following screenshot:

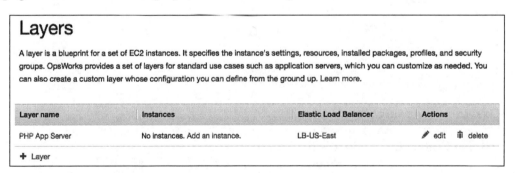

Summary

You now have been introduced to the concept of multistage environments and how those are represented in OpsWorks as something called stacks. We've gone over creating a stack, the available parameters, and how to work with functions that allow for stack management. We've also been introduced to layers, and we've gone over the Elastic Load Balancer including detail of how the ELB exceeds and where its limitations are when comparing it to technologies like HAProxy.

In the next chapter, we will discuss the second tier of OpsWorks known as layers. Layers are probably the most important and the most configurable of all areas in OpsWorks. Having a thorough working knowledge of layers will certainly lead to success with OpsWorks.

4
Layers – the Blueprint for Success

Layers are the most important and detailed component of OpsWorks. This chapter takes a look at layers in detail and explains why they're so important, as well as how they relate to stacks and instances. As you work through this chapter, you will discover that layers really are the configuration management feature of OpsWorks, and thus, they are the blueprint for success.

Configuring layers

As mentioned earlier, a layer is basically a blueprint for how an EC2 instance is put together. Layers define which packages and applications are installed, and how they are configured. OpsWorks provides a series of layers that are designed for common roles such as PHP and Ruby on Rails app servers, MySQL database servers, and so on. If the provided layers work for your needs, you can use them as they are, or you can customize them by using custom Chef recipes and assigning them to the appropriate lifecycle events.

It's also possible to create fully customized layers. Let's say you want a search layer; it's possible to build this by choosing the custom layer type and then defining all of the Chef recipes and OS packages required to bring an Elasticsearch cluster online. To date, the following layer types are available for selection:

- Load Balancer
    - HAProxy
    - Elastic Load Balancer

- App Server
  - ○ Static Web Server
  - ○ Rails App Server
  - ○ PHP App Server
  - ○ Node.js App Server

- DB
  - ○ MySQL

- Other
  - ○ Memcached
  - ○ Ganglia
  - ○ Custom

Every stack has at least one layer, and it's more likely that a stack will have several layers; all of which determine the stack's overall functionality. A typical stack will consist of a load balancer layer, app server layer, database layer, caching layer, and monitoring layer, but other layer types are required in several situations, and this is why the Custom layer exists.

We already have one layer from *Chapter 3*, *Stack it Up!* which is the PHP App Server, and this layer includes an Elastic Load Balancer. We now need to configure the PHP App Server layer so that it's tailored more to our liking and needs.

Make sure that you're on the staging stack we created earlier, and then click on **PHP App Server** under the **Layers** section. Now, click on the blue **Edit** button to the top right of the page and you should see a page as illustrated by the following screenshot:

Layer **PHP App Server**

Settings

Built-in Chef Recipes ⓘ

We have defined 20 built-in Chef recipes for your layer. Show »

Custom Chef Recipes ⓘ

If you want to use Custom Chef recipes you need to **configure cookbooks** first.

Elastic Load Balancing ⓘ

Elastic Load Balancer [LB-US-East   ÷]

Built-in Chef recipes

You should be aware by now from *Chapter 1, A New Way to Scale* that OpsWorks is at its core, a Chef-based framework. Because of this, built-in Chef recipes are required in order for the provided layers to function. If you click the **Show** link where it says **We have defined 20 built-in Chef Recipes for your layer**. You'll see all of the Chef recipes that are provided to get a PHP App Server up and running on OpsWorks.

If you are unfamiliar with Chef, it is a configuration management framework that allows a DevOps role the ability to run infrastructure as code. With Chef, all systems and deployments are pre-configured using a hierarchical framework of directories and files that are written using a Ruby domain specific language. At the highest level, Chef works with repositories, and inside repositories, there exists a multi-directory layout including something called cookbooks. Inside cookbooks are files which are known as recipes, and each recipe file contains a Ruby DSL which fetches, installs, and configures packages based on your requirements.

It's not an absolute requirement that you know Chef in order to work with OpsWorks. It's totally possible to build an entire infrastructure without any Chef knowledge; however, if you require any type of custom layer, Chef will more than likely become a requirement. If you're interested in learning more about Chef, head over to the Opscode website: `http://www.opscode.com`.

The following figure illustrates a typical Chef repository:

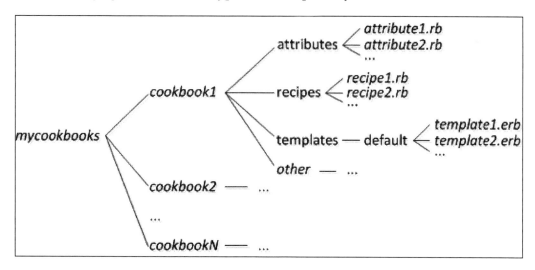

The top level of a Chef repository doesn't actually contain any Ruby recipes, attributes, or templates. Instead, what is required to exist is simply a list of folders with each folder representing a cookbook. Each cookbook folder contains subfolders for the respective Ruby scripts.

Now, there are several key things to mention here with the following figure, and the first is about the bold text (**Setup**, **Configure**, **Deploy**, **Undeploy**, and **Shutdown**):

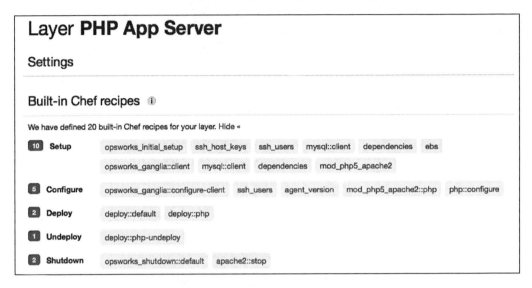

These items represent the lifecycle of an instance using OpsWorks and Chef recipes.

As you can see in the previous screenshot, the Chef recipes are staggered over each stage of the lifecycle. If you click on one of the recipes, you'll be taken to that recipe as it exists in its respective cookbook, which resides in the `opsworks-cookbooks` repository on GitHub. Examining the structure of these cookbooks and the Ruby code in the recipes is also a way to start learning Chef.

- **Setup**:

  The Setup lifecycle event runs on a new instance once it's been successfully booted. OpsWorks runs Chef recipes to set up the instance according to how its layer is configured. In our example, the Setup event of the PHP App Server layer installs SSH keys and users along a MySQL and Ganglia client, as well as some dependencies.

- **Configure**:

  The Configure lifecycle event runs on all of the instances in a stack when an instance either enters or leaves an online state. Let's say that the staging stack has instances php-app1, php-app2, and php-app3, and then you bring a php-app4 online. Once php-app4 has completed the Setup lifecycle event, OpsWorks will initialize the Configure event on php-app1, php-app2, php-app3, and php-app4. Now, let's say that you stop php-app1; OpsWorks will again initialize the Configure event on php-app2, php-app3, and php-app4. AWS OpsWorks will respond to Configure events by running each layer's Configure recipes. This action updates the configuration of all instances to reflect the current set of the existing online instances.

  The Configure event is a good time to re-generate configuration files. For example, if you have a load balancer configured and you add the instance php-app4 as mentioned earlier, OpsWorks will run the Configure event for all php-app instances, as well as for the load balancer. This is so that all instances are aware of the new addition and so that the load balancer can effectively distribute traffic as intended. This same action also happens when you remove an instance.

- **Deploy**:

  The Deploy lifecycle event happens when a deploy command is run; this command is designed to deploy applications and packages to application server instances. Instances will be triggered to run recipes, which deploy application code from repositories, or install and update package dependencies as configured at the instance layer.

  There are basically two types of deployments: **Application** and **Command**. The Application deployment is designed for deploying apps, and the Command deployment is designed for deploying package dependencies, updating Chef cookbooks, or executing incidental recipes and custom Chef JSON. This action allows you to update instance configurations where needed to accommodate newly deployed applications.

- **Undeploy**:

  The Undeploy lifecycle event happens when an app is deleted or with the goal of removing an app from application instances. When this action is triggered, instances are instructed to run Chef recipes that are designed to remove application versions and cleanup any related code, directories, and so on that would become superfluous.

- **Shutdown**:

  The Shutdown lifecycle event takes place after instances are instructed to be stopped, but before the instance is actually terminated. This time the window is no greater than 45 seconds, and it allows OpsWorks to run Chef recipes to perform tasks for removing an instance from the pool.

Custom Chef recipes

For the purpose of this book, you will be shown how to configure OpsWorks to use custom Chef recipes, where they should be stored, and how they can be updated, but we won't be diving into writing custom Chef recipes.

OpsWorks allows you to use custom Chef recipes in addition to the built-in Chef recipes. At this point in time, this is an extremely important feature, as it allows you to step outside the limitations of what OpsWorks provides when creating layers. As mentioned earlier in this chapter, if you wanted to build something like an Elasticsearch cluster, OpsWorks allows no way of doing this using the provided layer types. Because of this limitation, a custom layer would be required, and that custom layer would have to be instructed to use custom Chef recipes that are designed to install and configure Elasticsearch.

So, in order to use custom Chef recipes, we require a repository of Chef cookbooks that include the recipes. A typical repository could exist in a place such as GitHub, Bitbucket, an SVN repository, or even an HTTP or S3 archive. Using a Git-based repository is a great alternative as it provides a distributed and secure VCS model that allows for easy code updates and from multiple developers if needed. Let's look at a Git-based repository on GitHub as an example; of course, for this you'll need a GitHub account, and if you're unfamiliar with Git or GitHub, Pro Git is a great place to start: `http://git-scm.com/book`. Once you are familiarized with Git and how it works, you can open up a GitHub account to start working with it.

If we create a new repository on GitHub called `opsworks-cookbooks`, we can then start building our cookbooks and recipes in our local IDE, which can then be pushed to the GitHub repo. As illustrated earlier, the framework for a Chef repository includes cookbooks and recipes as illustrated again in the following figure:

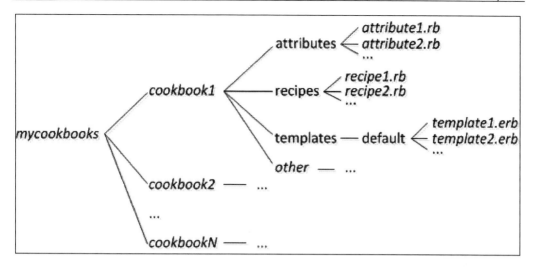

As you can see, at the top level would be the GitHub/Chef repository name (mycookbooks), and inside the repository is where any cookbooks you create will reside. Now, cookbooks don't just contain recipes; recipes are the scripts that do all the heavy lifting, but those recipes commonly function alongside things such as templates and attributes so that system and packages can be configured using variables and custom parameters.

As mentioned earlier, Chef cookbooks are ideally created using your local IDE, and by using certain Chef commands such as knife for creating cookbook frameworks. Once you have a cookbook created, it should ideally be initialized with Git, and then pushed to a remote private repository on GitHub.

 A very easy way of acquiring Chef cookbooks and adding them to your GitHub cookbook repository is to search and find them on the Opscode Community Cookbooks website, then follow their links to GitHub and fork them.

Once this task has been accomplished, it's time to configure OpsWorks for use with the custom Chef repository on GitHub, and for this to happen, we have to navigate back up to the staging stack. If you navigate back to the staging stack, click on the **Stack Settings** button, then click on **Edit**; you'll notice an item that says **Use custom Chef Cookbooks**, and this item should be set to **No** by default. If you slide this option to **Yes**, more options such as **Repository type**, **Repository URL**, **Repository SSH key**, and **Branch/Revision** become available. By default, Git is set as the option for **Repository type**, and if you are familiarized with Git, you should already be aware of what these settings mean and how to configure them.

The **Repository SSH key** setting allows you to add a public SSH key to your GitHub repository, then specify the private SSH key using this setting in OpsWorks. The reason for this is so that you can host your custom Chef cookbooks in a private and secured GitHub repo.

Let's navigate back to our layer and continue on with the layer settings. Click on the **Layers** link in the left navigation pane, click on **PHP App Server**, and then click on the **Edit** button. You should see a page as illustrated in the following screenshot:

Elastic Load Balancer

We've already gone through the setup of an ELB and have gone over several informational points that relate to what it's about and how it differs from HAProxy. You should see at this point that **LB-US-East** is available for selection with this layer. We can now move on to EBS volumes.

EBS volumes

EBS stands for **Elastic Block Store**, and although this storage technology is technically network attached, it acts as though it's direct-attached storage. This means that you cannot use two servers to share one EBS volume. If there is a requirement for shared network attached storage, S3 is the option by design with AWS.

Being that EBS volumes are treated as direct-attached storage; they are purposeful when used for things like database volumes, that is, MySQL, custom Elasticsearch, and so on. When creating an EBS volume, there are options for where the volume should be mounted, the RAID level, number of disks, and the size per disk. Multiple EBS volumes can be created per layer, and each instance that is a part of the layer will inherit this configuration. If EBS volumes are to be assigned to a high-performance SQL database system, it's important to use RAID 10 for speed and redundancy at this point.

Our example layer is a PHP App Server, and so no EBS volumes are required.

Elastic IPs

Elastic IPs are an OpsWorks extended feature of AWS, and are designed to be static IP addresses. Elastic IPs can be easily added and removed from instances. Each AWS account is allowed up to 5 EIPs, and if more are required, then a request must be submitted to AWS Support for justified provisioning. Being that 5 EIPs are allowed per account, these must be used with discretion. For example, an EIP is ideal to use for load balancers or other instance types that require a Host A DNS record. Again, because we're working with a PHP App Server layer that will have instances behind an Elastic Load Balancer, no Elastic IPs are required here.

OS Packages

OS Packages are a very convenient and important feature of layers within OpsWorks. Using OS packages, you can add any package type that is supported with your default operating system as defined in your stack. If Ubuntu 12.04 LTS is the default operating system, any package that you can install by default using apt-get or aptitude install, will be available for selection using the **Package name** setting.

If you start typing the name of a package, you should be presented with a list of package names that meet the keyword. When configuring layers, it's a good idea to add common packages such as the following:

```
gcc make automake autoconf curl-devel openssl-devel zlib-devel httpd-
tools apr-devel apr-util-devel sqlite-devel nmap wget mlocate elinks
postgresql-devel
```

These packages are often precursors to several other packages that any Chef recipe might require in order to be executed successfully. Of course, it's always wise to be prudent when selecting additional packages for installation; a little research can go a long way in avoiding potential problems with existing AWS scripts, functionality, and so on.

Security groups

Security groups are of course extremely important, as they provide the necessary security with what ports are accessible and from which sources. Fortunately, OpsWorks makes this easy for us, and will create a default security group for each layer that it can provide. In our case here, the default security group is called `AWS-OpsWorks-PHP-App-Server`, and it provides access to ports 22, 80, and 443 from the outside world. There are also other ports that are made open, but these ports are only accessible from other default security groups such as the `AWS-OpsWorks-Web-Server` and `AWS-OpsWorks-LB-Server`. OpsWorks pre-configures this for you so that if you create various app server and load balancer layers, each instance that's launched within these layers will have unobstructed access to communicate with the other instances. For this reason, each security group of these layers is allowed access to all ports of the other layer security groups.

The security groups that are selected and defined in OpsWorks directly correlate to the security group's navigation item in the EC2 section of the AWS Management Console. OpsWorks allows you to choose more than one security group for your layer, and if you require additional security groups, they will need to be pre-defined using the EC2 section. Once additional security groups are defined, they will be made available for selection within an OpsWorks layer.

The following figure shows the default configuration of the `AWS-OpsWorks-PHP-App-Server` security group as it's configured in the EC2 section of the AWS Management Console:

ICMP		
Port (Service)	**Source**	**Action**
ALL	sg-8035dbeb (AWS-OpsWorks-Web-Server)	Delete
ALL	sg-8635dbed (AWS-OpsWorks-LB-Server)	Delete
TCP		
Port (Service)	**Source**	**Action**
1 - 65535	sg-8035dbeb (AWS-OpsWorks-Web-Server)	Delete
1 - 65535	sg-8635dbed (AWS-OpsWorks-LB-Server)	Delete
22 (SSH)	0.0.0.0/0	Delete
80 (HTTP)	0.0.0.0/0	Delete
443 (HTTPS)	0.0.0.0/0	Delete
UDP		

IAM instance profile

The **IAM instance profile** is an OpsWorks extended feature of AWS Identity Access Management. If you are familiar with IAM, then you already know that IAM works with JSON formatted scripts to allow permission to areas of AWS resources. In this particular case, the IAM instance profile enables you to give your instances access to AWS resources that you might have created.

When the staging stack was first created, a default IAM instance profile called `aws-opsworks-ec2-role` was automatically set up by OpsWorks. This is convenient; however, this default role has no policy, and thus no permissions.

If you are developing applications that have a requirement to make use of other AWS resources such as S3 buckets, RDS databases, and so on, it is a good idea to construct IAM policies in advance that allow this access, so that you can then select the policy as an IAM instance profile. The following example of a JSON formatted IAM policy that allows access to other AWS resources such as EC2, S3, and RDS is listed below:

```
{
  "Version": "2012-10-17",
  "Statement": [ {
    "Effect": "Allow",
    "Action": [ "ec2:*", "s3:*", "rds:*", "iam:PassRole"],
    "Resource": "*"
  }
  ]
}
```

Auto healing

Auto healing is an excellent feature of OpsWorks and is something that provides disaster recovery within a stack. All OpsWorks instances have an agent installed which not only works to install and configure each instance using Chef, but to also update OpsWorks with resource utilization information. If auto healing is enabled at the layer, and one or more instances experiences a health-related issue where the polling stops, OpsWorks will heal the instance. When OpsWorks heals an instance, it first terminates the problem instance, and then starts a new one as per the layer configuration. Being that the configuration is pulled from the layer; the new instance will be set up exactly as the old instance which has just been terminated.

When auto healing is enabled at the layer, any attempt to shut down or terminate an instance outside of OpsWorks, such as using the EC2 console, or the command line interface, will trigger OpsWorks to automatically heal the instance. If you need to shut down an instance when auto healing is enabled, make sure you do so using the OpsWorks console only.

Another item to be aware of is with respect to EBS volumes. During the auto healing process, OpsWorks will re-attach any EBS volumes that were attached to the unhealthy instance. If you decide to delete an EBS volume using the EC2 console, OpsWorks will replace the EBS volume automatically, but it will not replace the data.

MySQL layer

We will be working with MySQL in the chapters ahead, so for the sake of this book, let's move forward with creating a layer for it.

If you navigate back to the layers section by clicking on the **Layers** link in the left navigation pane, you should already see the **PHP App Server** layer. Click the **+ Layer** hyperlink below it to add a new layer, choose **MySQL** as the **Layer type**, then set the **MySQL root user password** to be 8ePO2O8E0UHG91975I3k. Now make sure that **Set root user password on every instance** is toggled to **Yes**, then click the Add Layer button.

We've now successfully created a layer for MySQL.

Summary

You should now have a pretty good understanding of what a layer is in OpsWorks, and how it relates to stacks and instances. We've covered the different types of layers, how the Chef framework works with respect to built-in Chef and custom Chef recipes and we've also covered ELB, EBS, EIP, OS packages, security groups, IAM instance profiles, auto healing, as well as the MySQL layer. It's easy to see how layers really are the workhorse of OpsWorks; it's where the majority of configuration ties together.

The most important step to take from here will be to learn Chef. As mentioned before, knowing Chef is not mandatory, but if having a heterogeneous network of systems and applications is the end goal when using OpsWorks, then learning how to work with Chef will certainly be a must.

In the next chapter, we will focus on the third level of OpsWorks called instances. Instances inherit the majority of configuration that is made with stacks and layers, and they are the technology that runs software packages and applications. Properly managing instance configuration will ensure that an infrastructure and application will be able to scale both timely and effectively.

5
In an Instance

This chapter discusses the various instance types available to OpsWorks, as well as how to configure arrays of instances for the benefit of auto scaling in response to traffic demands. Throughout this chapter, we will configure three distinct instance arrays which will respond to traffic demands in different ways. Each instance array has its time and place within AWS OpsWorks.

Instance types

In the previous chapter, we finished discussing layers in detail. As mentioned at the end of *Chapter 4*, *Layers – The Blueprint for Success*, most of the configuration that has been made to stacks and layers is inherited by the instances. That being said, it's important to do some research on what type of traffic you will need to initially support, and to also plan for how and when you will need to effectively scale your application and infrastructure. Scaling can require several actions in order to happen, and of those actions, horizontal and vertical scaling methods are important to strategize. Understanding the different instance types will allow you to scale your infrastructure and applications while managing costs and expectations in response to traffic volume.

Considering that OpsWorks is an integral service to AWS, almost all EC2 instance types available to AWS are available to OpsWorks. The list of EC2 instance types available include, but are not limited to (because of ever-evolving features) the following:

- **Micro**:

  Micro instances, otherwise known as the t1 class, are the lowest cost instance type, and they provide a short burst of up to two ECUs, 615MB memory, and very limited I/O. Micro instances are ideal for low traffic sites, blogs, and small administrative applications. For the purpose of this book, we will be making use of Micro instances for cost saving reasons.

- **Standard 1st Gen.**:

  Standard 1st Gen. instances, otherwise known as the m1 class, are general purpose, and are some of the first instances which were available to AWS. These instances will most likely be phased out relatively soon, but for now, they are ideal for things such as small and midsize databases, data processing, encoding, and caching.

- **Standard 2nd Gen.**:

  Standard 2nd Gen. instances, otherwise known as the m3 class, are also general purpose, but they provide the option for a greater number of virtual CPUs and thus provide higher performance than the m1 class.

- **HighMEM**:

  HighMEM instances, otherwise known as the m2 class, are memory optimized instances that are well suited for high performance databases as well as caches such as Memcached. Memory optimized instances have the lowest cost per gigabyte of RAM among all EC2 instance types.

- **HighCPU**:

  HighCPU instances, otherwise known as the c1 class, are compute optimized instances which are well suited for applications that require high compute power. Compute optimized instances have a higher ratio of CPUs to memory, as well as the lowest cost per CPU among all EC2 instance types.

- **HighIO**:

  HighIO instances, otherwise known as the hi1 class, are storage optimized instances, and they provide optimized direct-attached storage options for applications with specific disk I/O and storage capacity requirements. A typical use-case for the hi1 class would be NoSQL databases such as Cassandra and MongoDB, as well as scale out transactional databases such as MySQL and PostgreSQL.

- **HighStorage**:

    HighStorage instances, otherwise known as the hs1 class, are also storage optimized instances. They provide tens of terabytes of storage, have high network performance, and offer a throughput performance of up to 2.6 GB/s. Use-cases for the hs1 class include Hadoop and other clustered file systems.

Instance scaling types

OpsWorks instances can have one of three scaling types: 24/7, time-based, or load-based. In order for time-based or load-based instances to work effectively, at least two 24/7 instances will be required. Having two 24/7 instances makes complete sense, being that you would not scale an infrastructure and application without using a load balancer, and you would not have a load balancer with less than two instances.

24/7 instances

24/7 instances are the default scaling type of OpsWorks. When you first create an instance under the **Instances** category in the left navigation pane, the instance will assume a 24/7 scaling type. This means that the instance will be active 24 hours a day, 7 days a week, unless it's manually shut down.

 Remember, instances should only be shut down from within the OpsWorks Console to avoid any erroneous rebooting as a result of auto healing.

If you plan on building an auto scaling array behind a load balancer, at least two 24/7 instances are required.

Time-based instances

Time-based instances allow you to schedule auto scaling by having OpsWorks start instances at predictable days and times. If you assume that traffic will be higher during the week, you could have OpsWorks scheduled to start a certain number of instances, then to decommission those instances on the weekends. Another use for this would be in the way of utility, where you might require more compute power for scheduled tasks to be run, such as those that are short-running or related to heavy workload.

Load-based instances

Load-based instances allow you to scale your instance array by adding instances when you experience traffic spikes, and stopping instances when the traffic subsides. There are load metrics which you can define in order to accomplish this type of auto scaling, such as configuring OpsWorks to start instances when the average CPU utilization exceeds 80 percent, and then also to stop instances when the average CPU utilization falls below 30 percent. These types of parameters can be defined as you see fit for CPU, memory, and load.

Adding instances

Now that we've gone over both the instance and scaling types, let's move forward with creating 24/7 instances.

Adding 24/7 instances

If you've been following along until this point using OpsWorks, you should be at the Instances page as illustrated in the following screenshot:

Instances

An instance represents an EC2 instance. Each instance belongs to a layer that defines the instance's settings, resources, installed packages, profiles and security groups. When you start the instance, OpsWorks uses the associated layer's blueprint to create and configure a corresponding EC2 instance. Learn more.

PHP App Server

No instances. Add an instance.

You can add more layers to this stack.

Click on the **Add an instance** link to add an instance. If your stack and layer were created properly, you should see php-app1 as the **Hostname, Medium (c1.medium)** as the **Size** (this is not configurable in the stack or layer), and **us-east-1c** as the **Availability Zone**. Set the **Size** to **Micro (t1.micro)** and click on the **Advanced** link.

After you click on the **Advanced** link, you should be presented with several options for configuring the instance, as illustrated in the following screenshot:

Host name	php-app1
Size	Micro (t1.micro)
Availability Zone	us–east–1c
Scaling type	⦿ 24/7
	○ time-based
	○ load-based
SSH key	AWSKeyPair–Virginia
Operating system	Ubuntu 12.04 LTS
Architecture	⦿ 64bit
	○ 32bit
Root device type	○ Instance store
	⦿ EBS backed

We are going to leave all of the options as their default. As mentioned earlier, the first two instances will have a scaling type of 24/7. The **SSH key** is set as the default key which you should have created as mentioned in *Chapter 3, Stack it Up!*. The **Operating system** should be **Ubuntu 12.04 LTS**, as configured at the stack level. The **Architecture** should be set to **64bit**, and this is especially important when choosing Micro instances, as they have the least amount of physical resources; 64bit will provide a bit of a performance boost. The **Root device type** should be set to **EBS backed**, which will provide faster boot times and persistent data when stopped and started again.

Once all of these settings are in place, click on the **Add Instance** button. When an instance is first added, it's put into a stopped state. The reason for this is for additional control, or so that you have the option of adding several instances, which you can bring online all at the same time. You should now see a page similar to the following screenshot:

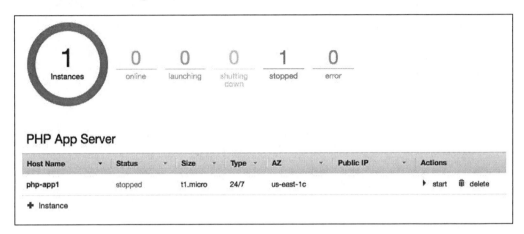

Now that we have one instance, let's proceed by creating a second instance. Click on the **+ Instance** link and provide the same settings as you did when creating the first instance. When that's done, click on the **Add Instance** button, and you should now see php-app1 and php-app2 instances in the **Instances** console.

You should also be able to see a **Start All Instances** button to the top right of the page. If you click on this button, both instances will be initialized and launched. We actually don't want to click on this button just yet, because we haven't defined any applications; nor have we defined any auto scaling arrays, which we will do next.

Adding load-based instances

We're now going to add a load-based instance array for auto scaling purposes, and this is where the fun starts to happen with OpsWorks, particularly when traffic is increased against an application.

To add a load-based instance array, click on the **Load-based** link in the **Instances** category of the left navigation menu. You should see a page similar to the following screenshot:

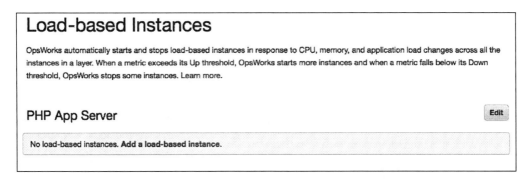

The first thing that should be configured here are the parameters for load-based auto scaling. In order to do this, we need to click on the **Edit** button, which should display information as illustrated in the following screenshot:

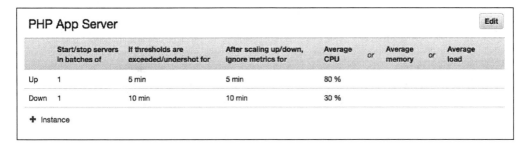

Defining these parameters accurately can take some testing and adjusting, and that can only really be done once the infrastructure is deployed and simulated traffic is directed at the application. Let's go over the options before configuring any of the settings.

Start/stop servers in batches of

This setting tells OpsWorks how many instances you would like to have started once the threshold of average CPU, memory, or load are exceeded. This is useful if you have experienced traffic spikes that are too demanding for just one instance at a time to be launched. If this is the case, having two or three instances launched at a time might work best for your situation. Again, this type of understanding can only be achieved after you know exactly what instance types you will use, that is, Micro, Standard 2nd Gen, HighCPU, and so on; this can also depend on how the database, caching, and application respond in concert. For the purpose of this exercise, we'll stick with the default of 1.

If thresholds are exceeded/undershot for

This setting defines how long OpsWorks will wait after exceeding a threshold before starting or stopping instances. For example, you can configure this so that CPU utilization must exceed the threshold of 80 percent for at least 15 minutes. The benefit of this is that it allows you to ignore brief traffic fluctuations when it comes to auto scaling. Again, depending on what your traffic is anticipated to be, it might make more sense to have a shorter threshold than the given example of 15 minutes.

After scaling up/down, ignore metrics for

This setting tells OpsWorks how long it should wait after starting or stopping instances before monitoring metrics again. This gives you the ability to allow enough time for started instances to come online, or stopped instances to shut down before determining whether the instances within the layer are still exceeding a threshold.

 This is a very important setting. If this setting is improperly configured, real-world traffic could lead to an excessive number of instances booting up, and this could not only cost maintenance time, but also money.

Average CPU, memory, and load

The average CPU, memory, and load settings are the thresholds that you set, to which OpsWorks responds by starting or stopping instances.

By default, OpsWorks provides 80 percent up and 30 percent down for CPU, with a server batch of 1, with 5 and 10 minute threshold windows, and 5 and 10 minute metrics windows. By using the default settings, if a layer experiences 80 percent CPU utilization across all instances for 5 consecutive minutes, one additional instance will be started. Once the instance is started, OpsWorks will ignore metrics for a period of 5 minutes. After the 5 minutes have elapsed, OpsWorks will begin to monitor the metrics again, and if the CPU threshold still exceeds 80 percent for the layer, another instance will be launched, and so on. The reverse action will take place according to the parameters in the **Down** row if CPU utilization falls below 30 percent.

One thing to note with automatic load-based scaling is that it does not create new instances. Automatic load-based scaling only starts and stops those instances which you have already created, and that are in a stopped state. This is yet another area where testing needs to be done in advance. Advance testing will allow you to anticipate the number of instances that are required to handle the traffic you expect to experience, and then provision new systems accordingly.

For the purpose of this section, let's leave the defaults as they are, then set the **Load-based auto scaling enabled** switch to **Yes** and click on the **Save** button. You should now see a page similar to the following screenshot:

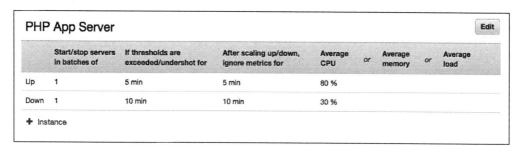

Now that the load-based parameters are set, let's go ahead and add a load-based instance. Click on the **+ Instance** link and follow the same steps as outlined under the previous Adding 24/7 instances section in this chapter.

If everything went according to plan, you should have one new instance which should be named php-app3. The php-app3 instance should have a stopped status, and it should be represented by a 1.micro that exists in the us-east-1c availability zone. If this is the case, you should be seeing a page similar to what's displayed in the following screenshot:

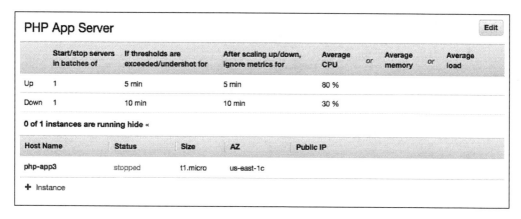

MySQL instance

In *Chapter 4, Layers – The Blueprint for Success,* we created a database layer for MySQL, and now is the opportunity to add an instance for MySQL. Click on the **Instances** link in the left navigation pane; you should see a PHP App Server section that shows three PHP app servers, and another MySQL section with no instances.

Click on the **Add an instance** link. Adding a MySQL database instance is the same process as adding a PHP App Server instance; the only thing that really changes here is the hostname, which should default to being db-master1. Once that is completed, click on the **Add Instance** button to add the instance.

Summary

In this chapter, we've taken a look at the different instance types that are available to OpsWorks, as well as the various scaling types that can be applied to those instances. We've also defined a load-based scaling array and have added instances to it for auto scaling response to increased traffic.

In the following chapter, we will cover the next level of OpsWorks called **apps**. Apps are where you define a series of parameters that involve your applications so that OpsWorks can automatically deploy and configure them on the instances that are started.

6
Bring the Apps!

This chapter focuses on how OpsWorks can deliver applications to instances developed for them. There are many different approaches to developing applications, and this chapter will discuss a very modern approach which makes use of a distributed version control system, as well as how that approach integrates with AWS OpsWorks.

Continuous integration

Continuous integration is a term that is commonly mentioned in the same context as other terms such as **configuration management** and **continuous delivery**, and is also a term that is often a part of both. Continuous integration is a very important component in application development, as it allows for distributed submissions of code from multiple developers, and provides easy versioning and excellent control when developing applications.

Distributed is the new centralized

If you're familiar with version control systems (VCS), then you've probably heard of, and maybe even have worked with a system called **Git**. Git is a distributed version control system that was developed by the creator of the Linux kernel, Linus Torvalds. Using Git, developers can create branches of their codebase, and then add and manage features, hotfixes, and releases to the application in a secure and controlled manner. We will not be diving into Git (as it's a lengthy technical subject), but I do suggest reading Pro Git, available at `http://git-scm.com/book`.

GitHub

So, what if you have initialized a Git repository and you've been working with Git using feature, hotfix, release branches, and so on...where do you go from here? In order for Git to be truly useful, the codebase must be pushed to a centralized repository hosted somewhere on the Internet. Fortunately, there are services out there that offer Git-based hosting, such as GitHub. Once application code is pushed up to a repository on GitHub, it can then be contributed to by several developers. If you don't already have a GitHub account created, I encourage you to do so by going to `https://github.com`.

Local IDE (Integrated Development Environment)

A local IDE is of absolute importance for successful application development. For the most part, an IDE is really a software program that provides source code editing, build automation, and debugging tools. There are many IDE programs to choose from, such as Aptana Studio, Komodo IDE, Eclipse, and Zend Studio. Think of an IDE as the complete set of tools that assist in a developer's production, and with that being said, you'll find the following items to be very efficient for web application development:

Mac OS X, MySQL Server, MySQL Workbench, iTerm, Sublime Text, and Git.

Together, these software programs form a great local IDE that can produce well-formatted code for any language, while providing automatic builds and database interaction. Having a well put together local IDE can go a long way when forming a development team, so that everyone is on the same page and has the same understanding of how applications are being produced.

Adding an app

We've gone over some methods for having an efficient implementation of a local IDE, and the local IDE is the development stage of a multistage environment. In *Chapter 3, Stack it Up!*, we discussed multistage environments, including development, staging, and production. We are currently working on the staging environment using OpsWorks; the local IDE is the development environment, and we will get to the production environment in the coming chapters.

Let's move ahead with adding a demo application to our staging stack in OpsWorks. In your staging stack, click on the **Apps** link in the left navigation pane; this will take you to the apps section of OpsWorks. Once you've made it there, click on the **Add an app** link to navigate to the **App New** page.

OpsWorks provides a very quick and simple method for accessing your application code. Let's go over all of the settings on the **App New** page to get familiarized.

Settings

- **Name**:

  This setting is simply a field for naming the application what you want it to be. For the demo application, name it OpsWorks Book Demo.

- **App type**:

  This setting tells OpsWorks what codebase your application is developed in. Ruby on **Rails**, **PHP**, **Node.js**, **Static**, and **Other** are the available choices. The OpsWorks Book Demo application is made using PHP, so choose that as your app type.

- **Document root**:

  The document root allows you to specify a document root for your application, should it require customization. The default for it is public, and this is what works well with OpsWorks. It also follows the MVC pattern, should you be using an MVC framework. Leave this field blank.

Application source

- **Repository type**:

  The repository type allows you to specify which VCS repository type you're using, and what the URL is for it. Options for VCS repository types include **Git**, **Subversion (SVN)**, **HTTP archive**, and **S3 archive**. There is also an option for a custom repository type for repositories like Bazaar. However, OpsWorks will not automatically fetch application code when using the custom type; instead, Chef cookbooks and recipes must be written to accommodate this functionality. Select **Git** for the repository type.

- **Repository URL**:

  This is simply the URL that you will use for the repository. Being that the demo app we will deploy is hosted at GitHub, add the following address: `https://github.com/todd-vivisurf/opsworks-book-demo.git`.

  > One thing to note here is that the field placeholder specifies an old read-only URL format that GitHub no longer supports. Make sure to use the HTTPS version.

- **Repository SSH key**:

  The **Repository SSH key** is optional and is what you will want to use when setting up private repos for secured application code that you don't want the world to see or contribute to as open source. For the purpose of this exercise, we can leave this field blank, as the repository code is publicly available. If this repository were private, a private SSH key would be required.

- **Branch/Revision**:

  With respect to Git and GitHub, the Branch/Revision setting tells OpsWorks which branch to deploy from your repository. If you're familiar with Git and branching models, you'll know that a Git repository can have several working branches of the same codebase. Typically, a Git repository will consist of at least a master branch and a develop branch. The develop branch is what developers pull down to their local IDE to work on. The develop branch is then merged into the master branch once all work is satisfactory; therefore, the master branch is the deployable main line of code. Enter `master` as the **Branch/Revision**, and make sure it's lowercase.

Add domains

- **Domain name**:

  The **Domain name** field allows you to tell OpsWorks what domain names and URLs your application should support. These values are then used in the web server configuration so that they can properly direct traffic to the application directory to serve up the code. For the purpose of this exercise, you can leave this blank. We will test the application against the public DNS record as provided by AWS when an application instance is started and the demo app is deployed.

SSL settings

- **Enable SSL**:

  The Enable SSL switch is on by default, and it allows you to specify SSL certificate information for SSL termination with your application. If you recall in *Chapter 3, Stack it Up!* we discussed in detail the ELB and how it can handle SSL termination. Enabling your application to handle SSL termination along with the ELB will provide full end-to-end encrypted traffic. For the purpose of this exercise, we will set this switch to No, but we will continue to discuss the SSL-enabled options.

- **SSL certificate**:

  The **SSL certificate** field requires that you specify the Base64-encoded X.509 certificate (.crt) file of your certificate chain.

- **SSL certificate key**:

  The **SSL certificate key** field requires that you specify the Base64-encoded RSA private key file of your certificate chain.

- **SSL certificates of Certification Authorities**:

  The **SSL certificates of Certification Authorities** are an optional field, but in some cases it will be required depending on your SSL certificate provider. Providers such as GoDaddy will issue an intermediate certificate so that the .crt file and .key files are bundled with the GoDaddy trusted root certificates. This ensures maximum browser and server coverage to avoid common SSL errors.

As mentioned under **SSL Settings**, we will not be using SSL for this exercise, so make sure to toggle the **Enable SSL** switches to the Off position. You should now be looking at a screen similar to the following screenshot:

If your settings are all correct as per the previous screenshot, go ahead and click on the **Add App** button to add the app. If you've successfully added the app, you should now be looking at a screen similar to the following screenshot:

Deploy, edit, and delete

We've now stepped through the settings and creation of our demo application with OpsWorks. Of course, we still have to deploy the application, and there's always the possibility of things changing such as repositories and their configurations, modifying domain names, enabling SSL, and so on. Sometimes there's even the need to delete an app and start all over again, or just simply because the app is no longer needed.

This is where the deploy, edit, and delete actions come into play with OpsWorks, and as you can see in the previous screenshot, there are links to support these actions.

Deploy

The deploy action is designed to perform running tasks that can deploy or undeploy an application's codebase to application servers, as well as maintenance-related tasks such as starting, stopping, and restarting the web server.

If you click on the **deploy** link, you'll be taken to the **Deploy App** screen, and this is where all of the supported actions can be initiated. There's also the ability to provide comments for the actions, as well as custom Chef JSON, in the event that you need to pass variables to the stack that should override any preset custom Chef JSON.

If you've already clicked on the **deploy** link, you should see a screen similar to the following screenshot:

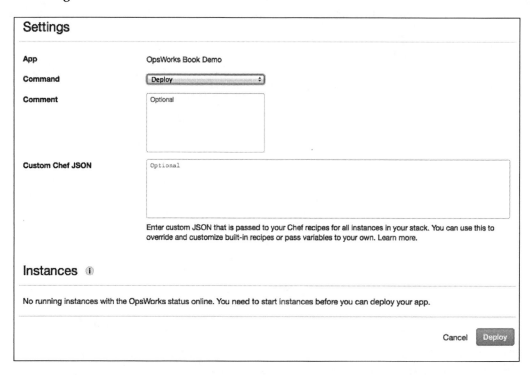

You should also see that the **Deploy** button is disabled, and this is because we have not yet started any instances. Obviously, if there are no instances, then there's nothing to deploy to.

Edit

If we had made a mistake during the initial configuration of our app, we can just as easily click on the **edit** link to return to the app configuration to make any corrections that are necessary.

Delete

If we are totally unsatisfied with this application configuration and would like to completely remove it, clicking on the **delete** link will accomplish this.

Now that we've gone over what apps are available to OpsWorks, including the vast majority of the configuration settings, let's put a deployment to the test.

The first thing that we're going to want to do is to access the Instances Console in OpsWorks, and we'll make sure that we're in the correct place by clicking on the **Instances** link in the left navigation. Once you're there, you should see a screen similar to the following screenshot:

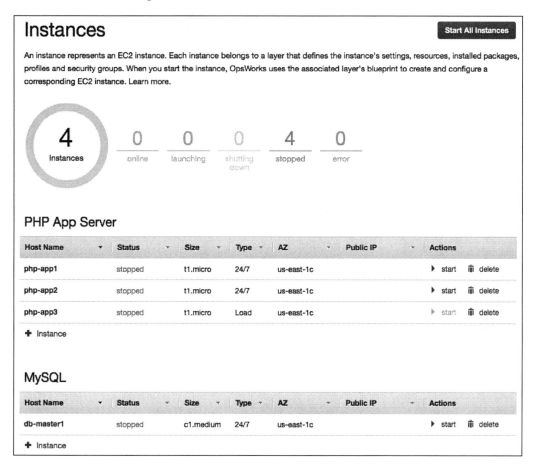

Notice the entire instance types that are listed here; you should be seeing the same. We can now move ahead and start the **php-app1** instance by clicking on the **start** link in its corresponding row. Now, there's something that you might experience here that will seem out of the ordinary. As the **php-app1** instance is booting up and going through its setup and configuration steps, you may notice that the **php-app3** instance also begins to start up and go through its setup and configuration. This will be because we're working with t1.micro instances, and these instances have limited CPU resources. If you recall earlier in this chapter, we configured the load-based array to scale up if the layer exceeds an 80 percent threshold, and this can happen with the t1.micro instances during configuration. This is actually a good thing to have happen at this point, because it proves that the load-based auto scaling array is working properly. Once the **php-app1** and **php-app3** instances have finished going through setup and configuration, and after 5 minutes have passed, the **php-app3** instance should quickly return to a stopped state.

> Because the demo app was already created, OpsWorks will have automatically deployed the app during the instance setup and configuration. We will, however, continue to walk through the steps in deploying the application. This is important to know as this is how future updates to application code will make it to the instances.

Now, our **php-app1** instance should have a status of being online. If this is the case, let's navigate back to the Apps Console of OpsWorks by clicking on the **Apps** link in the left navigation pane. When you reach the Apps Console, click on the **deploy** link in the **OpsWorks Book Demo** row, and from here, simply accept the default settings which should only include the **php-app1** instance. Click on the **deploy** button. You should now see the deployment take place, and at the end of it, a green color coded status of **successful** should exist as illustrated in the following screenshot:

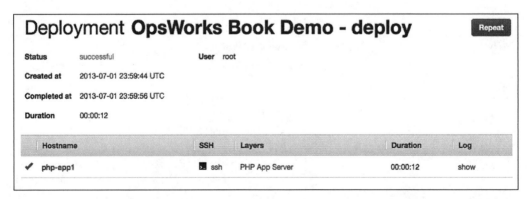

Here's where things start to get interesting, and if your deployment was not successful, make sure to review your configuration at the stack, layer, and app levels. We'll assume that your deployment was successful, so let's proceed by clicking on the **php-app1** link under the **Hostname** column of the deployment row.

Once you've clicked on the **php-app1** link, you should be presented with a page full of details surrounding the application instance, as well as network, security, and logging information. The page will look something similar to the following screenshot:

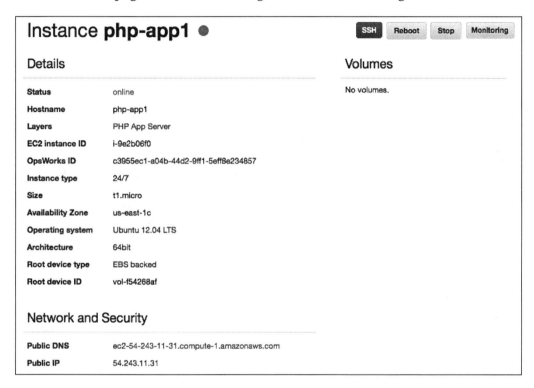

As you can see, there are several details that reflect the settings configured throughout the stack.

You should also be able to see the **Public DNS** and **Public IP** fields which are hyperlinked, and if you click on either of those, you should be presented with the demo application for this book as illustrated in the following screenshot:

> Because the database server has not yet been configured, it may take a minute for the PHP demo app to be displayed.

Now, you might say to yourself "Well this isn't much of an application," and you're right. We haven't set our database instance up yet. As you can see by the error on top of the table, it says **Connect failed: Can't connect to MySQL server on '127.0.0.7' (111)**.

The OpsWorks demo application also requires minor additional configuration to connect to the database host. Ideally, OpsWorks uses Chef to automate these types of configurations, which is a vast topic that requires a great deal of understanding in order to automate setup and configuration tasks such as this one.

What I'm going to recommend that you do next, is to ensure that the following has been performed:

1. You have a GitHub account. If you don't, open up a browser and navigate to `https://github.com` to create one.

2. Once you've logged into your account and authenticated against GitHub, you should then navigate to `https://github.com/todd-vivisurf/opsworks-book-demo`.

3. Fork the `opsworks-book-demo` repository by clicking on the **Fork** button. This action will create a public version of the `opsworks-book-demo` in your GitHub account.

4. Clone the new forked repository into the `webdoc` root of your local IDE with the following command: `git clone https://github.com/todd-vivisurf/opsworks-book-demo`.

5. Start your OpsWorks MySQL database instance so that you can get the Public DNS value for `dbconnect.php`.

6. Open up the `dbconnect.php` file in the `includes` directory of the GitHub cloned application on your local IDE and edit the indicated values to be what they should be. The username and password should already be correct; you just need to change the `$DB_HOST` values to the Private IP address of your MySQL server instance.

7. Commit the code using `git commit -a -m "updated dbconnect.php"`.

8. Push the code back up to your forked repository using `git push origin master`.

9. SSH into the MySQL instance using your AWS key pair and the Public IP value of the database instance. The command will look similar to this: `ssh -i AWSKeyPair-Virginia.pem ubuntu@54.242.154.39`.

10. Open up the `opsworks_book_demo.sql` file in the includes directory of the GitHub cloned application on your local IDE. Sublime Text 2 is a great choice for this.

11. Copy the entire contents of the file to the clipboard and save it as a new file on the command line of the database instance using the VI editor. Name the new file with the same filename of `opsworks_book_demo.sql`.

12. Import the `opsworks_book_demo.sql` file by using the following command: `mysql -u root -p opsworks_book_demo < opsworks_book_demo.sql`. You will need to supply the database password that's in the dbconnect.php file of the demo app.

13. Edit your Apps layer to reflect the newly forked GitHub repository in your account.

14. Re-run the deployment on the application.

Once these actions are performed, you should be able to click on the hyperlinked **Public DNS** of your **php-app1** instance with the results of the following screenshot:

OpsWorks Book Demo

PHP demo page for use with AWS OpsWorks

Title	Description	URL	View
Bootstraptor free KIT Twitter Bootstrap templates	WHAT IN THIS BOX Gradually accumulated some templates, we have decided to provide it for Bootstrap community. Free of charge to download a set of basic template build with Bootstrap framework on his popular base.	http://www.bootstraptor.com/	Go
Bootstrap Fireworks Toolkit	The original Bootstrap Toolkit for Adobe Fireworks. It contains all of the version 2.1 ui elements created as reusable vectors. Copy and Paste them over to your new Fireworks document to create your designs. Perfect for creating web apps!	http://www.fireworkstoolkits.com/	Go
How To Build and Customize Your Own Bootstrap Theme	A guide on quickly choosing the right colors for your bootstrap theme and how to efficiently build said theme. Also includes other resources and a list of unique sites built with Bootstrap	http://antjanus.com/blog/web-development-tutorials /how-to-build-your-own-bootstrap-theme/	Go
Bootstrap Infographic	A very nice interactive inforgraphic about Twitter Bootstrap	http://www.templatemonster.com/infographics /bootstrap-interactive-infographics.php	Go

Example courtesy of Todd Rosner from Vivisurf

View my profile on **Linked** in

As you can see, the demo application is now retrieving information from the database instance, and as a result, there is no longer a SQL error, and the table is populated with Bootstrap information and links.

Now, the next step is bringing this all together with the 2nd PHP App Server and the ELB. In order to do this, go ahead and start **php-app2**, and when that instance has completed its booting and setup, navigate back to **Deployments** using the left navigation pane and click the **Deploy an App** button.

> Make sure to click on the **Advanced** link under the **Instances** section of the **Deploy App** page, and uncheck the **MySQL** option. This will effectively tell OpsWorks not to deploy the app to the database server.

When that's done, click on the **Deploy** button. After the deployment is complete for both **php-app1** and **php-app2**, you will be informed by a green success status as seen by the following screenshot:

Status	successful	User	root
Created at	2013-07-03 04:35:42 UTC		
Completed at	2013-07-03 04:36:42 UTC		
Duration	00:01:00		

Hostname	SSH	Layers	Duration	Log
✔ php-app1	ssh	PHP App Server	00:01:00	show
✔ php-app2	ssh	PHP App Server	00:01:00	show

If you proceed to click on either of the **php-app1** or **php-app2** links, you'll be taken to their instance details page where you can click on the **Public DNS** link to verify that the application is working. Once this is verified, it's time to add the ELB back into the equation.

To add the ELB to the existing infrastructure and application, navigate to the **Layers** page by using the left navigation pane and then click on the **Add an ELB** link in the PHP **App Server** row. In the **Elastic Load Balancer** section, select **LB-US-East** for the load balancer and then click on the **Save** button.

To verify that the ELB is added and operational, navigate back to the Layers page again, and this time click on the **LB-US-East** link in the **PHP App Server** row. You will be taken to the settings page for the load balancer, where you can then verify its operation by clicking on the hyperlinked DNS name. From here, the demo app should display.

From here, the most logical step would be to create a **CNAME** record for the load balancer DNS Name, just to make things official.

Capistrano

An interesting point about OpsWorks is that it currently uses a specific Ruby Doman Specific Language (DSL) that is designed to assist with the deployment of application code in a multistage environment. The reason that I mention Capistrano in this chapter is because it's the framework that really performs all of the delivery of the code, and being that Capistrano is Ruby-based; it ties nicely into the Chef framework that OpsWorks is built upon.

If you've not heard of, or used Capistrano before, it's valuable to know about it because it's a diverse tool that not only can deploy application code, but also automate various system administration tasks; think of Capistrano as a very light-weight alternative to Chef. Chef has emerged as the stronger and more complete alternative for configuration management and so on, but nonetheless, OpsWorks makes use of both frameworks for configuration management and delivery of applications.

If you're interested in Capistrano for light-weight configuration management tasks that exist outside of any DevOps driven service, you can get started by going to `https://github.com/capistrano/capistrano`.

Summary

We've covered quite a bit of ground throughout this chapter, and hopefully you've been able to work through all of the steps involved. Application development software and methods such as IDE and Git are essential for any system that intends to scale, and coordinating local development with VCS hosting and the creation of apps is really the only way to achieve application deployments using OpsWorks.

In the next chapter, we will look at the monitoring features of OpsWorks, and how those features relate to both OpsWorks and AWS CloudWatch.

7
Big Brother

This chapter focuses on the monitoring component of OpsWorks, and how that monitoring service relates to the different areas of OpsWorks, as well as AWS CloudWatch. If you're already familiar with CloudWatch and what it can do, then you should be able to gather a quick and easy understanding of this chapter. If you are not familiar with CloudWatch, this chapter will provide a background, and it's recommended to get acquainted with the service using the CloudWatch Management Console and documentation.

Amazon CloudWatch

At the core of OpsWorks, the monitoring service is Amazon CloudWatch. It is the AWS service that provides monitoring and metrics for any AWS service which has that requirement. Using Amazon CloudWatch, a DevOps role can collect and track metrics for resources such as EC2, EBS, ELB, RDS, SNS, SQS, and so on, so that they can react quickly to keep those resources running. CloudWatch also provides the ability to monitor custom metrics which are generated by customer applications and services. This extends CloudWatch monitoring beyond just AWS resources, which in turn provides resource utilization, application performance, and operational health, for system-wide visibility.

Amazon CloudWatch has its own service section of the AWS Management Console, and if you navigate to the management console, you will be able to find and access CloudWatch by clicking on **Services** | **Deployment & Delivery** | **CloudWatch**.

One interesting feature of the CloudWatch Management Console that's also really helpful is the ability to define alarms and notifications for billing with AWS services. This allows you to be notified via SNS when your desired budget has been exceeded, so that you can monitor the financial status of your infrastructure elasticity.

OpsWorks monitoring

AWS OpsWorks uses Amazon CloudWatch to provide metrics-based information, which it summarizes for your convenience on the monitoring page. Using OpsWorks monitoring, it's possible to view metrics for an entire stack, a specific layer, or a specific instance. There are 13 one-minute metrics that provide an overview of the state of your instances, and all metrics are automatically collected, grouped, and filtered. With OpsWorks monitoring, you can start with a summarized overview of CPU, memory, and load for a stack, then drill down to specific layers and instances. All metrics can also be used to create alarms via Amazon CloudWatch.

Let's now take a look at the monitoring page of OpsWorks. If you have stopped your OpsWorks instances, go ahead and start **php-app1**, **php-app2**, and **db-master1**. Once those instances are running, click on the **Monitoring** link in the left navigation pane of OpsWorks.

Stack metrics

When you first access the monitoring page of OpsWorks, you'll be directed to the Monitoring Layers page where you'll see a stack view which has graphs relating to the layers you have defined within the stack. There are 4 graphs in total for each layer in the stack view: **CPU System**, **Memory Used**, **Load**, and **Processes**. By selecting the **24 hours** select list at the top right of the graphing area, time periods such as **1 hour**, **8 hours**, **24 hours**, **1 week**, or **2 weeks** can be selected for filtering the metrics over time.

The following for OpsWorks monitoring at the stack level is true:

- Graphs are updated every 120 seconds.
- The graphs display average values for layers that have more than one instance.
- Graphing time periods can be specified from 1 hour to 2 weeks.

The following figure illustrates the monitoring page in OpsWorks:

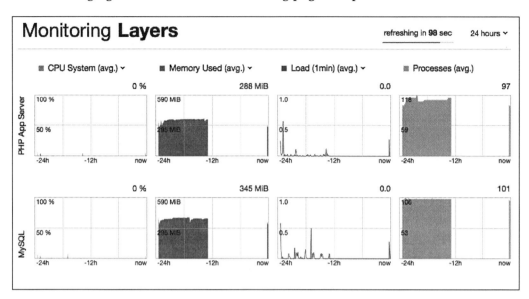

For each metric type, you can use the list at the top of the graph to select the particular metric that you want to view.

The **CPU System** graph ranges from 0 to 100%. This graph can display metrics for the time that the CPU is idle, the time it's handling user operations, as well as the time it's handling system operations, and when it's waiting for IO operations.

The **Memory Used** graph ranges from 0 to the total amount of memory. This graph can display metrics for the total amount of memory, the amount of memory in use, as well as the amount of swap space, and the amount of free memory.

The **Load** graph ranges from 0 to the current maximum value. This graph can display metrics for load averages over 1, 5, and 15 minute windows.

The **Processes** graph ranges from 0 to the current maximum value. This graph displays a single metric that includes the number of active processes.

Layer metrics

So, this is some pretty useful information at a high level. But what if we wanted to get more granular with the metrics to see what's going on with each instance? OpsWorks makes drilling down on the levels and metrics easy by simply clicking on the layer you want to see more information about.

Let's go ahead and click on the **PHP App Server** graphing layer. After clicking on the layer, you should see a breakdown of all of the instances within that layer, and each of these instances should have graphing for the same metrics as the layer did.

The following figure illustrates the layer metrics graph view:

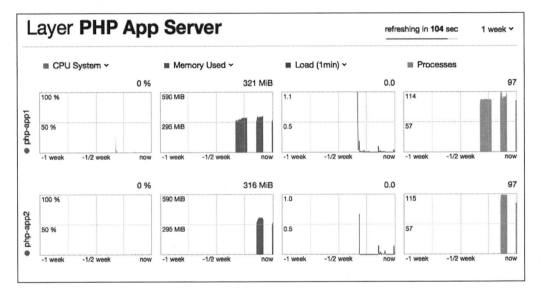

Instance metrics

Drilling down to monitor instance metrics is the same process as drilling down to monitor layer metrics; you just click on the instance you want to see extended metrics for and a new graphing view will be displayed. The instance metrics graphs are designed to summarize each metric type. To get exact values for a particular point in time, hover your mouse over a graphing area, and the boxed charts to the right of the graphing area will follow your movements. As the box charts follow your movements, each metric will change to display the resource usage in 2 second intervals. This feature is a great way to pinpoint resource utilization in AWS OpsWorks.

The following figure illustrates the instance metrics graph view:

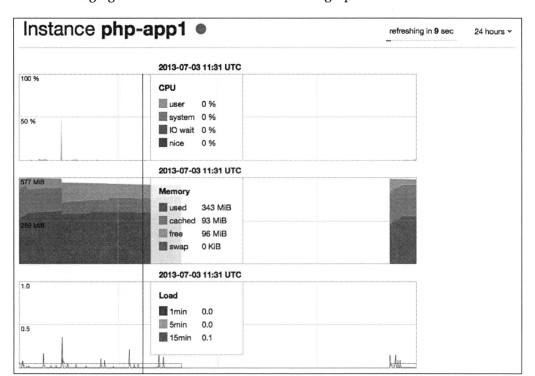

Summary

In this chapter, we've covered the ways in which OpsWorks provides monitoring for stacks, layers, and instances, and how CloudWatch is integrated. The OpsWorks graphing system has a clean and simple layout, and it delivers point-in-time views that are easy to navigate and easy to understand.

In the next chapter, we will take a look at Identity Access Management (IAM) and how it relates to OpsWorks. IAM is the service that will allow you to securely control access to OpsWorks and other AWS resources.

8
Access Control

Security is a major part of any Internet infrastructure or application. Without security, many organizations would fail within a short period of time due to a security breach. Of course, there are several moving parts to any infrastructure and/or application, and thus, there are many ways in which things can be secured.

This chapter takes a look at a security service that enables OpsWorks to be secured by controlling the areas that Developers, SysAdmins, and DevOps have access to.

Identity and Access Management

Identity and Access Management (IAM) is an access security service provided by AWS, which is their solution for user and group permissions. **AWS Identity and Access Management (IAM)** can securely control access to AWS services and resources for organizations' users. By defining, creating, and managing users, groups, and JSON-formatted policies, you can either allow or deny access to AWS resources for users where appropriate.

Secure by default

IAM is secure by default. In other words, that when working with IAM; if a user or group is created, those account types will not have access to any AWS resources until explicitly enabled through the creation of JSON-formatted policies.

Integration

IAM is integrated with almost every service of AWS, and it can provide very granular permissions through proper policy implementation. For example, using these policies, you can allow or deny access to the entire service sections of AWS, or you can allow and limit access to service functions such as terminating EC2 instances, deleting S3 buckets, creating ELB listeners, and so on.

JSON and IAM policies

JSON has been mentioned a few times throughout this chapter already, and if you're not already familiar with **JSON**, the acronym stands for **JavaScript Object Notation**. JSON is a text-based, open standard designed for human-readable data interchange, which is accomplished by representing simple data structures and associative arrays, called objects.

AWS chose JSON as the exchange format for IAM policies, which makes perfect sense, and using a simple and fast data exchange format works well for distributing policies throughout the AWS service types. Applying IAM policies to AWS resources works by binding them to something called **Amazon Resource Names**, or **ARNs**. ARNs are single line descriptors of specific areas of AWS resources. An example of an ARN would be `arn:aws:s3:::my_bucket/*`. This example supports an S3 bucket called `my_bucket`, and is something that you can build an IAM policy around to allow or deny access to it, as shown in the following example:

```
{
  "Statement":[{
  "Effect":"Allow",
     "Action":["s3:ListBucket","s3:GetObject","s3:GetObjectVersion"],
         "Resource":["arn:aws:s3:::my_bucket/*","arn:aws:s3:::my_
bucket"]
     }]
}
```

When working with IAM policies, there are a few approaches to consider:

- **Using a policy template**:

  IAM provides templates for policies, which are broad permission sets, and in effect, the templates can create roles such as admin, power user, read only, and so on. There are several templates to choose from, and this is the easiest approach, but also the least granular.

- **Using a policy generator**:

  IAM also provides a method for generating policies based on services, actions, and ARNs. Using this method, you can select a service to build a policy for, such as S3, then select an action such as list buckets, and finally indicate an ARN such as a bucket name. This approach provides a wizard-like interface and offers extensive granularity.

- **Creating custom policies**:

  Creating custom IAM policies has the most potential of the three approaches for granularity, but this approach offers no assistance in policy generation.

Whichever approach you create, each policy created will be applied to a group name that will be defined within the IAM Console. Once you've created a group and have defined the policies for it, you can then create users and add them to the group, which is a very common practice with user, group, and permission administration.

IAM users and groups

Let's go through creating an IAM group, as well as a user, and then walk through applying a policy. If you're currently in the OpsWorks Console, click on the **Console Home** icon. This icon is represented as an orange cube at the top left corner of the page. Once you're in the main AWS Management Console, click on **IAM** under the **Deployment & Management** category of the console. You should now be looking at the IAM Dashboard and there should be a button that says **Create a New Group of Users**. You should also be able to see a section of this page called **AWS Account Alias** that has a URL listed. Make sure to copy and record this URL, then go ahead and click on the **Create a New Group of Users** button.

After you've clicked on the button for creating a new group, you should see a modal window that is prompting you for the name of the group as illustrated in the following figure:

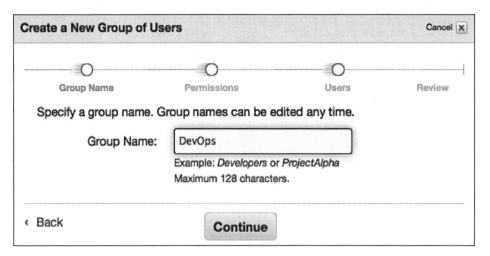

Name the group DevOps and click on the **Continue** button. You should now be presented with a modal window that provides you with all of the options for generating policies as we've gone over earlier in this chapter. The following figure shows the modal window of options:

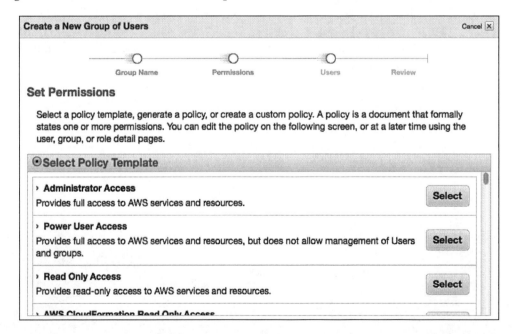

The modal window will default to the policy template way of applying policies. This is preferable for the purpose of this exercise, so for now, scroll down until you find the **AWS OpsWorks Full Access** template, and then click on the **Select** button.

After selecting the OpsWorks policy template, you'll see another modal window that will display the template's JSON-formatted policy. Here's where you can start to gain a real understanding of how IAM policies work. The template policy is listed in the following figure:

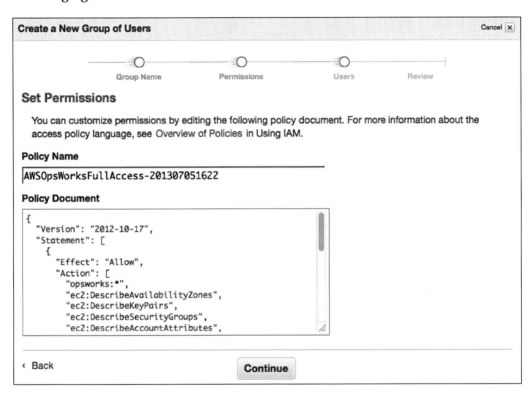

Click on the **Continue** button and you'll be presented with yet another modal window prompting you to create users, or to add existing users to this new group and policy. In the first username field, type in DevOpsAdmin. You should also see that there's a default setting for the creation of an access key for each user. This is important because it determines whether or not these IAM users will have the ability to access other services provided by AWS should they need to, and if this policy is modified further. The following figure illustrates these options:

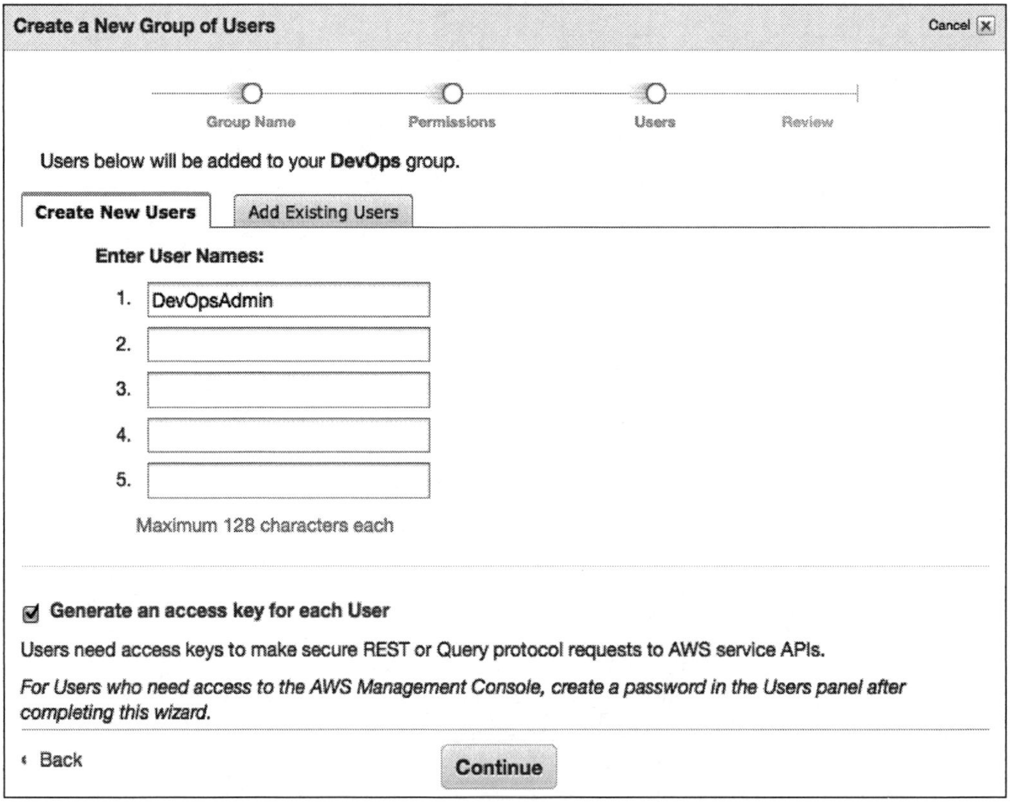

Click on the **Continue** button and you should be prompted to review the information. If you've made a mistake, you'll have the opportunity to make changes, as well. If all went well, click on the **Continue** button again, and you should be prompted with the ability to download the credentials, which you should go ahead and do.

From here, we're going to want to do two things. First, we'll want to assign a password to the new `DevOpsAdmin` user, and then we'll need to import that user into OpsWorks. To get started with this, click on the **Users** link in the left navigation pane of the IAM Console. You'll see the `DevOpsAdmin` user which you should click on to bring up the **users property** tabs. Click on the **Security Credentials** tab, then click on the **Manage Password** button and let IAM auto-generate a strong password for you. Either download or copy the password credentials somewhere safe. We'll use these credentials later to authenticate against the AWS Management Console and the OpsWorks Console.

OpsWorks and IAM

As mentioned previously, AWS OpsWorks integrates with AWS IAM. The same rules apply with IAM for OpsWorks as they would with any other service AWS provides. In other words, you can control user access throughout OpsWorks while at the same time limiting user access to other dependent services such as EC2, S3, ELB, and so on. An example of this would be permission to give users the ability to control instances in OpsWorks, while at the same time removing their ability to terminate instances using the EC2 Console or API.

In the exercise that this chapter demonstrates, so far there have been steps involved with creating a new IAM group, an IAM JSON policy via template, and a password protected user. We will now import the `DevOpsAdmin` user for use with the various areas of OpsWorks.

Navigate back to the OpsWorks Console by clicking on the **Services** link beside the orange **Console Home** cube, then click on the **OpsWorks** link under the **History** category. Once you're inside the OpsWorks Console, click on the **Permissions** link in the left navigation pane, and then click on the **Import IAM Users** link. Check the `DevOpsAdmin` user and then click on the **Import** button. You should now be seeing a page similar to the following figure:

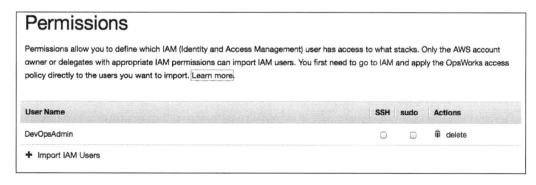

As you can see, the `DevOpsAdmin` user is now imported, and there are some management options that are available for use. The three options available are the following:

- **SSH**:

  This option allows a user to use the MindTerm SSH client to connect to instances in the stack. When users log in to an instance using SSH, they use their IAM user's short name. AWS OpsWorks auto-generates a short name based on the IAM username. OpsWorks does this by removing all non-alphanumeric characters, then by converting the username to lowercase. For example, the username `DevOpsAdmin` becomes `devopsadmin`.

- **sudo**:

  This option enables a user to have sudo privileges for instances in the stack. Logically, in order for sudo to work, the **SSH** option must also be checked. When both options are checked, OpsWorks will add the user's short name to the list of users with sudo privileges.

- **Actions**:

  The **Actions** column provides an ability to delete IAM users from the OpsWorks Console.

An item to note here is that importing an IAM user into the OpsWorks Console does transcend across each stack; however, the SSH and sudo options do not. If the SSH and sudo options are a requirement for an IAM user in each stack, they have to be explicitly set for each one.

Another item to note here is that in order for an IAM user to SSH into an instance, they will require a public key from an SSH keypair.

OpsWorks as an IAM user

Let's finish this chapter by testing our IAM policy and by setting a public SSH key for use with the MindTerm SSH client in OpsWorks. Sign out of AWS completely by clicking on your account name at the top right of the page and selecting **Sign Out**.

Signing in

Once you are signed out of AWS as your main account user, copy the AWS account alias URL that you recorded earlier and paste it into the browser address bar. Enter `DevOpsAdmin` as the username, and enter the password that IAM auto-generated for this user, which you should have also recorded.

If all went well, you should be signed in to the AWS Management Console. You should also be able to see all of the AWS available for selection. Even though we only provided access to the OpsWorks service for the DevOps user, you will still be able to click on all other service links which will bring up their respective console. The caveat here is that you will not be able to browse or manage any of the relating resources. However, you will be able to access, browse, and manage the resources in OpsWorks, because we provided full access to this service using the OpsWorks policy template.

Enabling SSH access via MindTerm

As the DevOpsAdmin user, navigate to OpsWorks from the AWS Management Console. When you reach the OpsWorks Console Dashboard, click on the **My Settings** link at the top right of the page, and you should be presented with the **My Settings** page as illustrated in the following screenshot:

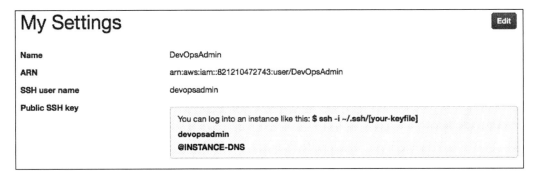

To enable SSH access using MindTerm or any other SSH client, click on the **Edit** button and add your public id_rsa.pub key, then click on the **Save** button. If you don't already have an RSA SSH key pair, GitHub has a nice tutorial on how this can be accomplished. The GitHub tutorial is available at https://help.github.com/articles/generating-ssh-keys.

Once this has been done, you should now be able to access the stack instances using your private id_rsa key including the DevOpsAdmin username and the Public DNS of the instance at hand.

Summary

In this chapter, we introduced AWS IAM to you, and we also demonstrated how IAM integrates with OpsWorks. From here, you should continue to explore IAM and how it all relates to OpsWorks.

In the next chapter, we will take a look at the Instance Agent CLI to show you how OpsWorks enables a DevOps role to use the CLI for running commands, viewing logs, and accessing agent reports.

9

Instance Agent Command Line Interface

Up until this chapter, we've seen just how practical AWS OpsWorks can be for building, deploying, and managing multistage environments. OpsWorks streamlines instance deployments via layered configuration management, and it streamlines application deployments by pulling source code from **Version Control System (VCS)** repositories.

OpsWorks also allows you to get under the hood, that is to say that there is not only the ability to connect to instances via SSH, but there's also a **command line interface (CLI)** that's exists with every OpsWorks agent installed. This chapter will take a look at connecting to an instance via SSH, as well as what you can accomplish when working with the instance agent CLI.

Connecting via SSH

Connecting to OpsWorks instances via SSH on the command line can be the same practice as it is for EC2. So long as the stack is configured to use the same default SSH key that's set up for use with EC2, you should be able to connect the same way you do for EC2. One nice thing about OpsWorks is that the service provides a couple of really quick ways to connect to instances that are started.

To connect to an instance using SSH via the OpsWorks console, you first need to access the **Instances** page using the left navigation. If you have running instances, and if your stack is configured to allow SSH for your user, you should see an option for SSH in the **Actions** column for each instance as illustrated in the following screenshot:

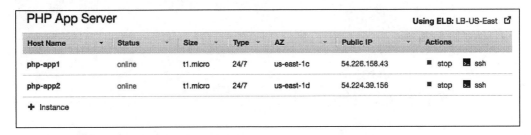

The SSH option under the **Actions** column is a hyperlink and when clicked on will take you to a page that provides supporting information and functionality for using the built-in OpsWorks methods. Of course, as mentioned in *Chapter 8, Access Control* you will need to be logged into the OpsWorks console as an IAM user, and in this case, it should be the user DevOpsAdmin. After you click on the **ssh** link in the **Actions** column, you should be seeing a page similar to following screenshot:

Connect from your browser using the Java SSH Client (Java Required)

In order to launch MindTerm, you need to enter the path to the private key located on your hard drive. AWS automatically detects the key pair name and public DNS for your instance.

Path to your private key

[   ]

```
Launch Mindterm
```

Connect directly

Directly connect to the instance using your terminal application.
ssh://ubuntu@54.226.158.43

Connect with a standalone SSH Client

1. Open an SSH client

2. Locate your private key file (AWSKeyPair-Virginia.pem). Your key file should not be publicly visible for SSH to work.

   ```
   chmod 400 AWSKeyPair-Virginia.pem
   ```

3. Connect to your instance using its IP address (54.226.158.43).

   ```
   ssh -i ~/.ssh/AWSKeyPair-Virginia.pem ubuntu@54.226.158.43
   ```

As you can see in the preceding screenshot, there are three separate methods to connecting to an instance.

Java SSH client connections

OpsWorks listed this option as the first one on the page; it is a browser based solution, and thus, you would think it's the fastest and easiest solution. There are a couple of reasons why this method might not actually be preferred.

1. This method is integrated into the browser. While this poses some convenience, it means that you won't be using an actual SSH client such as iTerm, and PuTTY which will give you a plethora of options for working on the command line.

2. Because this method is integrated into the browser, it requires Java to be installed and updated on your local IDE.

Connect directly

This method allows you to click on a provided hyperlink which in turn launches your default SSH client and logs you straight into the instance. Connecting directly makes use of your default AWS key pair and therefore, no additional configuration is required. This method is by far the easiest.

> Both this method and the browser-based `MindTerm` method do not make use of your AWS key pair. Instead, these methods use the public key which we added to the **My Settings** section for the DevOpsAdmin user in *Chapter 8, Access Control*.

Connect with a standalone SSH client

If your standalone SSH client is your default SSH client, then there should be no reason to use this method over connecting directly; it's the same thing only with extra steps. However, if connecting directly fails, the information provided here will help you manually connect to the instance. This method makes use of the same AWS key pair which is used for EC2.

For the purpose of this exercise and the sake of simplicity, let's go ahead and try the **Connect directly** method by clicking on the provided link. If this method presents some complication, try to use the **Connect with a standalone SSH Client** method.

After connecting directly, your SSH client should be automatically launched and you should be automatically logged in as user devopsadmin as illustrated in following screenshot:

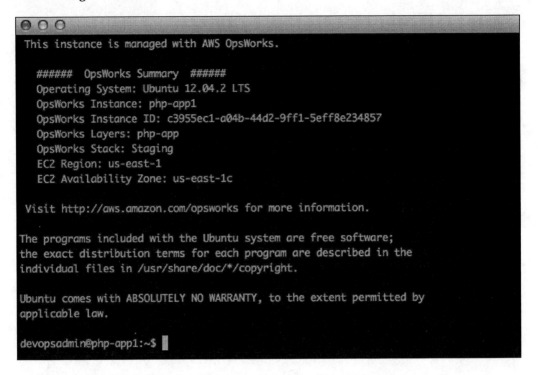

Instance Agent CLI

Now that we're connected to an instance via SSH direct connect, let's start working with the Instance Agent CLI provided by OpsWorks. As mentioned in the summary of *Chapter 8, Access Control* the Instance Agent CLI exists for running commands accessing and running Chef logs and recipes, as well as viewing instance and OpsWorks agent reports. With the Instance Agent CLI, there are seven categories with accompanying commands from which you can extract information and status about an infrastructure and application.

Reporting agent

The agent_report option of the CLI displays a report about the status of the agent installed on the instance from which the command is run. Information such as the last agent activity, agent status, and the agent version are all a part of the output.

The command for retrieving this information is **sudo opsworks-agent-cli agent_report**. The output for this command is illustrated in the following screenshot:

```
devopsadmin@php-app1:~$ sudo opsworks-agent-cli agent_report

AWS OpsWorks Instance Agent State Report:

  Last activity was a "execute_recipes" on Mon Jul 08 00:58:43 UTC 2013
  Agent Status: The AWS OpsWorks agent is running as PID 1025
  Agent Version: 125, up to date

devopsadmin@php-app1:~$
```

Getting JSON

The get_json option of the CLI outputs the configuration of the stack based on a lifecycle event such as setup, configure, deploy, and so on. The JSON-formatted output of the stack configuration is obviously quite lengthy, and it provides all of the details and options about the stack.

The command for retrieving this information is:

```
sudo opsworks-agent-cli get_json [activity] [date]
```

Instance reporting

The instance_report option displays extended information about the instance at hand. Information such as activity, status, version, stack, layer, instance, instance type, hardware resources, region location, and networking information are all available as output.

The command for retrieving this information is:

```
sudo opsworks-agent-cli instance_report
```

Listing commands

When run, the `list_commands` option will list the time for each activity that has been executed on this instance. Output for this command will show the date and time for each lifecycle event such as setup, configure, deploy, and so on.

The command for retrieving this information is:

```
sudo opsworks-agent-cli list_commands [activity] [date].
```

Lifecycle commands

The `run_command` option allows you to run a lifecycle event such as setup, configure, deploy, undeploy, start, stop, or restart. This option also allows you to schedule it at a particular time, and it provides the ability to pass JSON-formatted configuration options.

The command for retrieving this information is:

```
sudo opsworks-agent-cli run_command [activity] [date] [/path/to/valid/
json.file]
```

Show agent logging

The `show_log` option will tail the most recent OpsWorks agent log file. This option also allows you to filter and search the log file based on date and time, as well as by lifecycle event such as setup, configure, deploy, and so on.

The command for retrieving this information is:

```
sudo opsworks-agent-cli show_log [activity] [date]
```

State of the stack

The `stack_state` option is very similar to the `get_json` command option, in that it outputs a series of JSON-formatted data about the stack. The difference here is that this command is not based on any lifecycle event; instead, it simply outputs the state and configuration of the stack.

The command for retrieving this information is:

```
sudo opsworks-agent-cli stack_state.
```

Summary

In this chapter, we covered a couple of areas of OpsWorks which will certainly assist any DevOps role with infrastructure managing and reporting. It's obvious that connecting via SSH carries much importance for controlling processes and maintaining insight into the reliability and status of instances, but you might be wondering what else could be done with the Instance Agent CLI.

One idea that you might find interesting about the Instance Agent CLI includes the possibility of having each command run on a filtered schedule by way of a web application. The application could then output data in a responsive way, making it consumable by mobile devices.

Another idea would be to have a script periodically parse each command output, then notify a responsible person of any anomalies based on comparison and variance of the output.

Next up, we're going to take a look at what I believe to be the most exciting chapter of this book. We're going to use what we've learned to architect a multi-region infrastructure using OpsWorks and Route 53.

10
Multi-region Architecture

Throughout this book, we've covered almost every topic that relates to AWS OpsWorks, and we've also gone fairly deep into certain areas such as ELB versus HAProxy, how layers work, and how applications can be deployed.

We can now take the next big step by using the knowledge we've gained toward building a more scalable and redundant architecture, otherwise known as a **multi-region architecture**. To accomplish this, we're going to take a new look at the stacks and regions as they relate to OpsWorks. We'll also take a look into Route 53, which is Amazon's DNS web service.

Production stack

During the chapters of this book, we've focused on the local IDE as the development environment, and the staging stack as the staging environment. The most logical step from here would be the creation of a production stack for the production environment, and this is where OpsWorks can really pay off in terms of efficiencies.

Assuming that at this point the staging stack is tuned to where we want it to be for production use, let's navigate to the OpsWorks dashboard by clicking on the dashboard link at the top right of the OpsWorks Management Console. You should see your staging stack. If you click on the Actions link in the stack, you'll get a select list with the actions shown in the following figure, and as previously discussed in *Chapter 3, Stack it Up!*

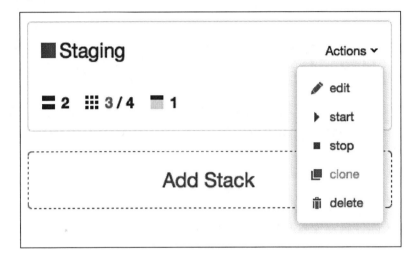

Notice in the preceding screenshot that the **clone** option is highlighted as being orange; this is what we're going to proceed with in cloning the staging stack into a production stack. So, we'll need to go ahead and select **clone** from the list of options.

Once the **clone** option has been chosen, you will be directed to the **Clone Stack** page which will allow you to change any parameters, should you need to. In our case, we simply want to change the name of the stack from **Staging copy** to **Production**. If you want, you can also change the default **Availability Zone** (**AZ**) to something different, and change the stack color to green for go.

 Cloning a stack provides the same layers, permissions, apps, and stack settings, but instances are not cloned during the process.

If all went well, you should be able to navigate back to the OpsWorks dashboard, where you will see the staging stack, as well as the production stack. Now what you can do is simply add instances to the layers in the newly created production stack. Once that's done, start the instances, then run your application deployments, and you should be ready to set your DNS records for production.

As you can see, the ability to clone stacks is not only effortless, but it's also very important in the way of consistency when building highly scalable infrastructures. Without the ability to clone stacks, settings could be misconfigured which would lead to lost time.

 One thing to be aware of with cloning stacks is that once they're cloned, any further updates will have to be done across every stack that's supposed to be the same.

Multi-region

So far, we've gone through how to create and configure stacks for both staging and production. We also know that AWS supports multiple availability zones for redundancy reasons. AZ redundancy is great, but what if an entire region or more than 50 percent of its zones failed, or became unstable due to cascading issues that spanned multiple technologies? This type of thing can happen with any cloud provider, and therefore it's really up to you to put as much intelligence into designing and protecting your infrastructure as possible.

Because there's still the potential for an AWS region to fail, it's logical to assume that taking things up a level higher by having redundant regions would be the way to go. This assumption would not only be correct, but it is also entirely possible using OpsWorks. As an example, what we might want to accomplish is a model that consists of the following (with a focus toward production):

Production stack created in the U.S. Virginia region:

- 1 x ELB
- 2 x 24/7 app servers
- An array of load-based auto scaling instances
- An array of replicated database servers
- All instances spread across the availability zones of Virginia

Production stack created in the U.S. Oregon region:

- 1 x ELB
- 2 x 24/7 app servers
- An array of load-based auto scaling instances
- An array of replicated database servers
- All instances spread across the availability zones of Oregon

You can probably see where this is going quite easily. We basically have two regions with Virginia and Oregon. At each of the regions there exists an identical infrastructure that supports load balancing and auto scaling application servers, as well as replicated database servers.

Seems pretty good so far, right? The great thing about OpsWorks is that we can simply create and refine one stack for staging, then clone that into production, then clone that production stack into another production stack and put it into a separate region.

Now, you might be thinking that this is all great, but how is the traffic going to be distributed to the different regions? Or maybe you're wondering about how region failover will work, and what handles that type of response? And what about when failover does occur; how does all of that extra traffic get absorbed in the other region? Well, this is where one of the best DNS services on the planet comes in, and that service is something that's provided by Amazon and is called Route 53.

Amazon Route 53

Amazon Route 53 is a highly available and scalable **Domain Name System (DNS)** that is one of the many web services available with AWS. Route 53 provides excellent functionality, scalability, and intuitiveness. Using Route 53, you can expect to receive the following qualities as they relate to DNS:

- **High availability and reliability**:

  Route 53 is backed by AWS's highly available and reliable infrastructure. The service offers each zone four name servers for redundancy and query routing optimization.

- **Scalability**:

  Route 53 is designed to automatically scale to handle very large query volumes. There are no settings or configuration for scaling DNS query traffic; Route 53 simply does this in the background for you.

- **Tight integration with other AWS**:

  Route 53 is designed to work well with other AWS. You can use Route 53 to map domain names to EC2 instances, S3 buckets, CloudFront distributions, and other AWS resources. When creating new DNS records for use with other AWS resources, the records are instantly propagated.

- **Simplicity**:

  With the AWS self-service sign-up, zones and records can be set up in minutes using the Route 53 console or the available API.

- **Excellent performance**:

  Route 53 makes use of a global anycast network of DNS servers. With Route 53, users will be routed to the most optimal location based on topology and network conditions. Low query and record update latency are desirable features that Route 53 offers.

- **Inexpensive**:

  Route 53 maintains the same "pay for what you use" model that follows all AWS, and there are no up-front costs or usage commitments. At $0.50 per zone per month, and at $0.50 per million queries per month, the service is virtually free.

- **Security**:

  Route 53 offers the ability to be integrated with IAM, and by doing this, it's possible to create JSON-formatted policies so that you can control access to zones and records.

- **Flexibility**:

  Route 53 offers features to assist with high-level traffic routing. Routing policies such as simple, weighted, latency, and failover allow Route 53 to go above and beyond typical DNS systems by allowing you to control how your traffic is routed to its AWS endpoints. Route 53 also offers AWS endpoint health checking, which is a great solution when paired with a failover record policy.

The previously listed points include much sought after features when it comes to a DNS system, and Route 53 has them in spades.

OpsWorks and Route 53

Now that we've covered multi-region configuration with OpsWorks, and we've gone over some excellent features of Route 53, let's tie the two together in a scenario to properly enable traffic distribution to the regions.

We know that having infrastructure and applications deployed in two separate regions gives us redundancy, but how do we get traffic to balance to the separate regions? As previously mentioned, Route 53 goes beyond typical DNS services, and by using routing policies, Route 53 can balance traffic across multiple regions.

Simple routing policy

At the most basic level, Route 53 provides a **simple** routing policy. This policy simply routes traffic in a round robin fashion to the values listed within the record. This is otherwise known as **DNS round robin**, and if you have an ELB in more than one region, you can specify them both inside a single DNS record, and Route 53 will automatically balance the traffic load using round robin.

Weighted routing policy

Another routing policy provided by Route 53 is **weighted**. This policy allows you to apply weighted values to identical records. Let's say you have two regions, each with an ELB. Using the weighted policy, you could apply a weight value of 1 to record www.domain.tld that points to one region's ELB, then create another identical record, give it the value of 4 and point it at the other region's ELB. Route 53 will recognize a total weighted value of 5, and will direct traffic to the first region's ELB 1/5th of the time, and the other region's ELB will receive traffic 4/5ths of the time.

Latency routing policy

The **latency** routing policy provides the ability to direct traffic to a region with the lowest latency. Once two or more latency-based record sets with matching names and types are configured, Route 53 will use network latency and DNS telemetry to choose the closest region to where your users are coming from.

Failover routing policy

The **failover** routing policy provides the ability to direct traffic based on healthy resources. By creating basic HTTP or TCP-related health checks, Route 53 can be configured to direct traffic to both regions until one is unhealthy, after which point all traffic would be directed to the healthy region. You can also use this policy to direct all traffic to one region, and have the other as a cold standby to be used only in the event of failure. There's also the ability to mix and match when it comes to the failover routing policy.

So, as you can see, there are a variety of options for balancing and routing traffic to infrastructure and applications as they exist across multiple regions. Each option has its strength, so it's very important to consider traffic routing as you plan to scale.

In the scenario provided by this book, where we have two U.S. regions each with the identical infrastructure and application, and where each infrastructure supports auto scaling of the application tier, the routing policy option to choose would be failover in an active-active configuration . This would effectively load balance the traffic to both regions, and if one region suffered a failure, all traffic would be directed to the healthy region. Being that auto scaling is configuring in OpsWorks, the healthy region's infrastructure would simply auto scale to meet the demand of the additional traffic.

Summary

In this chapter, we've discussed how completing a multistage environment by quickly cloning the staging stack into a production stack can be accomplished. We've also covered what the next most logical step is in web-scale architecture using OpsWorks; this is accomplished by cloning additional stacks and placing them in separate AWS regions.

In addition to stack cloning, this chapter has also provided information about the qualities and benefits of Route 53. By covering some of the most prominent features of Route 53, this chapter has addressed the different ways in which DNS policies can be used to effectively route traffic to AWS resource endpoints, and how these policies can work to complete a multi-region architecture.

Venturing deeper into Amazon Route 53 and all of the features it provides is highly recommended. You'll soon agree that this integrated DNS web service is of the utmost importance when bringing web-scale to your infrastructure and application using AWS.

Index

Thank you for buying
Learning AWS OpsWorks

About Packt Publishing

Packt, pronounced 'packed', published its first book "Mastering phpMyAdmin for Effective MySQL Management" in April 2004 and subsequently continued to specialize in publishing highly focused books on specific technologies and solutions.

Our books and publications share the experiences of your fellow IT professionals in adapting and customizing today's systems, applications, and frameworks. Our solution based books give you the knowledge and power to customize the software and technologies you're using to get the job done. Packt books are more specific and less general than the IT books you have seen in the past. Our unique business model allows us to bring you more focused information, giving you more of what you need to know, and less of what you don't.

Packt is a modern, yet unique publishing company, which focuses on producing quality, cutting-edge books for communities of developers, administrators, and newbies alike. For more information, please visit our website: www.packtpub.com.

About Packt Enterprise

In 2010, Packt launched two new brands, Packt Enterprise and Packt Open Source, in order to continue its focus on specialization. This book is part of the Packt Enterprise brand, home to books published on enterprise software – software created by major vendors, including (but not limited to) IBM, Microsoft and Oracle, often for use in other corporations. Its titles will offer information relevant to a range of users of this software, including administrators, developers, architects, and end users.

Writing for Packt

We welcome all inquiries from people who are interested in authoring. Book proposals should be sent to author@packtpub.com. If your book idea is still at an early stage and you would like to discuss it first before writing a formal book proposal, contact us; one of our commissioning editors will get in touch with you.

We're not just looking for published authors; if you have strong technical skills but no writing experience, our experienced editors can help you develop a writing career, or simply get some additional reward for your expertise.

Amazon Web Services: Migrating your .NET Enterprise Application

ISBN: 978-1-849681-94-0   Paperback: 336 pages

Evaluate your Cloud requirements and successfully migrate your .NET Enterprise application to the Amazon Web Services Platform

1. Get to grips with Amazon Web Services from a Microsoft Enterprise .NET viewpoint

2. Fully understand all of the AWS products including EC2, EBS, and S3

3. Quickly set up your account and manage application security

Oracle Enterprise Manager Cloud Control 12c: Managing Data Center Chaos

ISBN: 978-1-849684-78-1   Paperback: 394 pages

Get to grips with the latest innovative techniques for managing data center chaos including performance tuning, security compliance, patching, and more

1. Learn about the tremendous capabilities of the latest powerhouse version of Oracle Enterprise Manager 12c Cloud Control

2. Take a deep dive into crucial topics including Provisioning and Patch Automation, Performance Management and Exadata Database Machine Management

3. Take advantage of the author's experience as an Oracle Certified Master in this real world guide including enterprise examples and case studies

Please check **www.PacktPub.com** for information on our titles

ISBN 978-1-78217-110-2

53299